Yellow
139

Blue
260

More GREAT DESIGN

USING 1, 2, & 3 COLORS

Purple
547

Yellow
139

Blue
260

COPYRIGHT

ISBN 0-942604-44-X
Library of Congress Catalog Card Number 94-076992

Distributors to the trade in the United States and Canada:

F & W Publications
1507 Dana Avenue
Cincinnati, Ohio 45207

Distributed throughout the rest of the world by:

Hearst Books International
1350 Avenue of the Americas
New York, New York 10019

Published by:

Madison Square Press
10 East 23rd Street
New York, New York 10010

Designed and edited by Supon Design Group, Inc.

Printed in Hong Kong

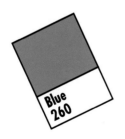

Blue
260

More GREAT

Blue
311

Purple
547   Yellow
139

Blue
260

Green
360

DESIGN
USING 1, 2, & 3 COLORS
SUPON DESIGN GROUP

ACKNOWLEDGMENTS

Project Director
Supon Phornirunlit

Communications Director
Wayne Kurie

Art Director
Supon Phornirunlit

Project Manager
Linda Klinger

Jacket Designer
Andrew Dolan

Design Editors
Andrew Dolan
Richard Lee Heffner
Supon Phornirunlit

Book Designer
Pat Taylor

Writers
Linda Klinger
Wayne Kurie

Support Staff

Andrew Berman	Michael LaManna
Dianne S. Cook	Paul Peddrick
Jacques Coughlin	Usha Rindani
Steve Delin	Apisak Eddie Saibua
Mimi Eanes	Deborah N. Savitt
Anthony Fletcher	

Desktop Publisher
CompuPrint, Washington, D.C., USA

Photographers
Barry Myers
Oi Veerasarn

CONTENTS

INTRODUCTION

Designers create artwork much like Picasso painted pictures: "I paint objects as I *think* them," he said, "not as I *see* them." What we as an audience see is the graphic artist's interpretation of business, commerce, reason, and reality. Objects and form and line take on personality through placement, turn, and, of course, color.

Color is an essential artistic element that finds its source in light. Commercial art — built on components that include color — finds its success largely in the mood, style, and tone that evolves from the potency of color. Excellent use of color is rarely accidental. A carefully thought-out process, color application can be used to soothe (blue), energize (red), or act as a neutral, soft backdrop to a more zestful shade. Color in the hands of a designer is malleable, and is transformed by choice, contrast, and amount. Good design often does not depend on the specific hue, but on its selective use. In our industry, we consistently find extraordinary work using a surprisingly small number of colors. This collection of graphic art continues a tribute to the talented designers who excel in this technique that started with the book *Great Design Using 1, 2, & 3 Colors.*

Swiping a page with a paintbrush is not usually the way color is used in design. It is the range of color intensity and its contrast to the background that brings the variety to the piece. Color variations can be created with texture on top of paint, the pattern into which the hues are regulated, the original angle of the stark silhouette or the line-drawn illusion. Just as a successful black-and-white photograph depends on the contrasts between brightness and darkness, softness of shadows and harshness of lines, the commercial artist sculpts his or her products — colorless — first, then explains the intention and infuses life with tints and tones.

The public is often enticed too readily by color. We need to be retrained to recognize how limiting colors in design can also produce magnificent, dramatic results. Interestingly, some of the work illustrated in this book was motivated less by budget than it was by designer's preference. In fact, we've seen the effectiveness of some simple designs lessened by adding too much color. From a budget standpoint, however, this is good news for many firms today. Burdened by years of weak economies, international corporations started tightening their belts in the early 1990s, initiating the acceptance of a new concept of frugality and sensible spending that replaced the lavishness of previous decades. Some firms were forced into budget consciousness. Few upstart companies, however, have ever entered the marketplace — then and now — with a large cache of money with which to promote themselves. The trend for using fewer colors — and, hence, a smaller design budget — has conveniently seemed to fit in with the times. In fact, many of the professionals in the industry admit to enjoying the challenge of keeping prices down and the puzzle of making more with less.

As our recognition of some of the best results that came from this challenge, this book was developed from thousands of entries from 36 countries around the world. The number of the submissions and their high quality made the selection process difficult; we still had numerous contenders for publication after we made the first cut. Readers will note that the entries included in this publication include organizations well known to the graphic community, as well as fresh new faces.

An editorial panel of art directors reviewed and evaluated all entries for several criteria. Of course, in this competition, exceptional use of color was the critical element. Then our immediate impressions were considered to determine whether the piece should be included in this volume. The public's anticipated perception of the work — including its effectiveness in achieving its goals, whether the proper connotation had been formulated, and the successfulness of its market orientation — was also considered. In addition, we also carefully reviewed whether the piece delivered its message directly and precisely. Pieces that meandered in their communication ability, however good they were otherwise, could not be considered exceptional in the business arena.

As always, although the process is time-consuming and complicated, we complete competitions such as this treasuring the wealth of concepts and radical views, especially from fledgling firms that have the skill to "think objects" a new way. We enjoyed finding both complexity and simplicity that still aroused strong sensibilities, and marvelled at the absolutely unique ways designers have found to speak to the world. We always learn something from these competitions, and come away with a fresh, new perception about our industry, and increased motivation to try something different.

The first volume, *Great Design Using 1, 2, & 3 Colors,* showed techniques used to stretch the effect of design. This book has discovered even newer techniques and showcases them here. Again, paper stock can and will provide an unexpected source of color; in fact, several studios actually combine different colors or textures of paper to produce unconventional effects. Handstamping, hand lettering, manual cutting, and photocopying can now create looks never before achievable for so little cost. In addition, for very small print runs,

you'll find examples of solutions printed directly from the laser printer and saddle-stitched by hand. We were especially impressed with print campaigns built of several components that used two colors for each piece, but varied the selection of the two colors for each separate element. The result, when all the campaign pieces were combined and displayed together as a unit, was a wonderfully colorful campaign combination.

As always, to those designers you will meet in this book and to those entrants whom we could not include, thank you for your participation in this competition. We especially appreciate your willingness to share your work with your peers; we have found it a delightful experience to become acquainted through design with such a vast pool of talented individuals. Surely this publication would not exist without you. And if you are interested in being considered for our next publication, please complete the postcard in this book and send it to us.

We wish you the best in your business endeavors, and hope this volume introduces you to many new ways to represent your world.

Supon

Supon Phornirunlit is owner of Supon Design Group, Inc., where he serves as creative director and art director. Since founding the company in 1988, he and his design team have earned almost 500 awards, including recognition from every major national design competition. His studio's work has appeared in publications such as *Graphis, Communication Arts, Print, Studio* and *How.* Supon has served on the board of directors of the Art Directors' Club of Metropolitan Washington and is currently on the board of the Broadcast Designers' Association. Supon and SDG have been featured in numerous magazines. He also regularly speaks at various organizations and schools.

ABOUT COLOR MATCHING

After the release of our first volume, *Great Design Using 1, 2, & 3 Colors*, we received some letters from designers interested in knowing the exact manufacturer colors and numbers that were used in the book. They requested that, in our next volume, we print the numbers of the chips used in each design so that they could experiment with similar applications.

Due to copyright restrictions and the technique used in printing, we regret that our books do not include trademark colors. Our publications are printed using a four-color process on a four-color press. This process builds the entire range of colors from four hues. What appears in our publications, then, are not actual trademark colors, but a very close match to them. In order to use specific manufacturer processes when printing full-color publications, we would have to print hundreds of definitive colors — an economic and organizational nightmare — to associate precise color chips with the design. When publishing books of our scope and magnitude, this option is simply not feasible.

For those interested in precision, you'll find the color chips we have used are similar approximations of the colors represented in your own manufacturer color key books. Colors can be closely matched by placing a vendor's chip beside our printed "chips" under white light.

THE BEST OF
1·2 & 3
COLORS

Gray
409

Yellow
125

Brown
485

Title: DogStar Print Awards Self-Promotion
Design Firm: DogStar Design, Birmingham, Alabama, USA
Art Director: Rodney Davidson
Designer: Rodney Davidson
Illustrator: Rodney Davidson
Copywriter: Rodney Davidson
Client: DogStar Design

I was working late one night on a logo when an old college roommate called to say he was getting married. After we talked, I started thinking about this song he used to sing, "I'll Sail Upon the Dog Star." I did a quick sketch of what I thought a Dog Star might look like and crawled into bed at 2 a.m. The next day, I showed my sketch to a few people and it was well received. One person even put in a request for a T-shirt—the ultimate endorsement. At that point, I knew my search for a logo was over. And that's the well thought-out marketing strategy behind DogStar Design.

DOGSTAR

DOGSTAR DESIGN AND ILLUSTRATION

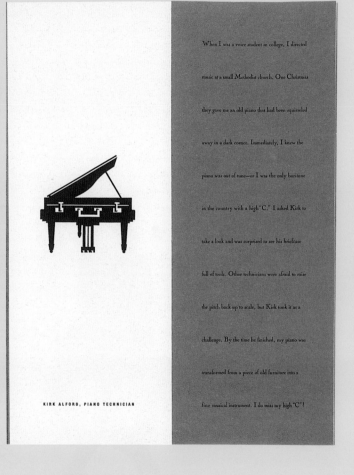

When I was a voice student in college, I directed music at a small Methodist church. One Christmas they gave me an old piano that had been squirreled away in a dark corner. Immediately, I knew the piano was out of tune—or I was the only baritone in the country with a high "C." I asked Kirk to take a look and was surprised to see his briefcase full of tools. Other technicians were afraid to raise the pitch back up to scale, but Kirk took it as a challenge. By the time he finished, my piano was transformed from a piece of old furniture into a fine musical instrument. I do miss my high "C"!

KIRK ALFORD, PIANO TECHNICIAN

This is an extraordinary work completely produced on a laser printer with construction paper, bound by a piece of threaded elastic, and housed in a homemade envelope. This piece, whose paper gives the illusion of texture, was motivated by several factors, including a low budget and Rodney Davidson's realization that every logo he had included in the brochure had a story behind it. He decided to share those stories. The ship illustration was scanned in on a computer, then a text program was brought in to create the text box. Color choice was determined by the sheets of construction paper Davidson happened to have around the studio that day. He put together a dummy, and was actually surprised the hues worked so well together. Davidson also wanted a design that would accomodate typing on the envelope instead of a sticker. The envelopes he found to house his piece were too expensive, so he made his own. Davidson has freelanced in graphic design for over a decade, but he admitted waiting many years to do a self-promotion. Trained as an opera singer, Davidson is now committed to a successful commercial art career.

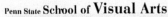

Penn State School of **Visual Arts**

volume**1**, number**1**, Fall 1993

Dear **Friends** & **Alums,**

I hope you will enjoy this, our first ever School of Visual Arts newsletter. It is long overdue and we have a lot to catch up on. Plans at present are to get subsequent editions to you annually. **Fourteen years have passed** since the Department of Art Education merged with the Department of Art to form the SVA. During this period there have been many changes in the facilities and programs of the School with more to come over the next several years. **The School of Visual Arts** presently occupies all or parts of several campus buildings. The Visual Arts Building, the School's primary studio-classroom-office structure, is located close to the Creamery. It is connected to the **Palmer Museum of Art** which is undergoing a 5.7 million dollar expansion (pictured above) designed by noted architect, Charles Moore. **The former Crafts Building,** now called the Arts Cottage, is the current home of art education. Classroom and studio spaces remain in portions of Chambers Building and on the second floor of the Arts Building. We are in the process of **renovating the Patterson Building,** one of the older brick "Ag Hill" buildings across from the Museum, for SVA use. Completion of these renovations in the spring of 1994 will mark the end of an era for art education in Chambers. At that time, all remaining studios and classrooms there will move to Patterson which will also house a well-equipped Macintosh teaching CAD lab and a "high end" College research CAD Lab. **The SVA administrative offices will move** to Patterson as well, creating space for a large, much needed seminar room in the Visual Arts Building. Although the moves will not increase overall square footage, they will bring the various components of our program physically closer together and make the School's available space more useful. **Over the last decade enrollment** of undergraduate students in our two programs, studio art and art education, **has grown tremendously.** It is now approaching **500 majors,** the largest number in our history. Demand by non-majors for SVA courses is also unprecedented. However, as we continue to struggle to accommodate the resurgence of student interest in the visual arts we are increasingly confident of a bright future. **Many of the School's most senior faculty members,** with whom large numbers of alumni studied, have retired over the past ten years. Although their presence is missed we have been fortunate to recruit a number of able and dedicated newer faculty who are carrying on the School's **tradition of excellence.** We are taking the opportunity in these pages to acquaint you with some of their activities along with those of faculty whose names may be more familiar. **I want to thank the hundreds of alumni** who answered my letter or returned the questionnaire for your tremendous response. Your notes and comments brought back many wonderful memories to those of us who reviewed the feedback. I trust that you will understand that the newsletter staff, because of the volume and length of your responses, may have been able to include only small bits and pieces of the information you submitted. However, an effort has been made to include something about everyone who returned the form. **We are very proud** of your many achievements and hope to formalize some events on campus in the near future to entice you back to share your memories and accomplishments in more detail. We also plan to seek your input as we shape our future. **Sincerely,**

James Stephenson, Director
School of Visual Arts

View of the Palmer Museum of Art.

View of patterson building.

Title: "Artsword" Newsletter
Design Firm: Sommese Design,
State College, Pennsylvania, USA
Art Director: Kristin Sommese
Designer: Kristin Sommese, Jim Lilly
Client: Pennsylvania State University, School of Visual Arts

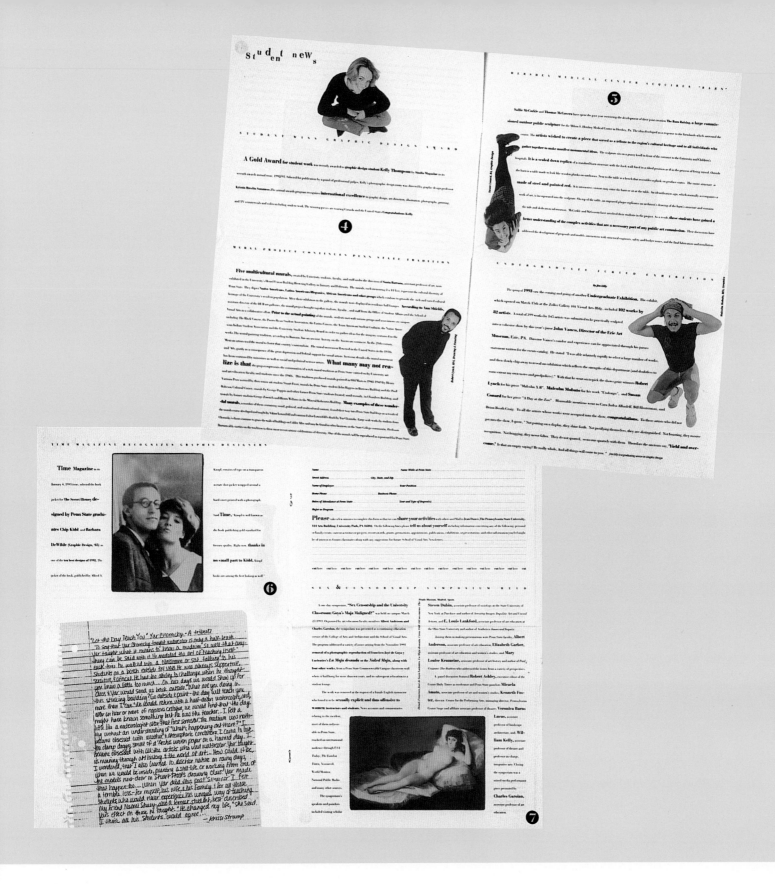

Sommese Design wanted this newsletter to appeal to all of its Penn State audience — alumni, faculty, staff, and students — without appearing too trendy. As an alternative to black-and-white photos, they chose somewhat neutral colors that they felt would make the faces look friendly. They also liked the effect of localized color behind the halftones while keeping it out of the type, and looked for hues that would be unusual to combine underneath images. The result: photos that look dimensional on the page. A small budget was also a factor; Sommese and Lilly (Sommese's former student) took the photographs themselves,

and accepted the project on a pro-bono basis, which offered considerable freedom. Some of the better effects were "happy accidents." While laying out color copies of the images, one fell into place upside-down, adding a level of fun and energizing the whole spread. Another "mistake" was the cover's volume and number display, which was the result of selecting only a portion of the whole word on the computer when changing type size. But when they allow things to simply happen regardless of the original intent, states Sommese, sometimes extraordinary things occur.

Title: Vintage Dallas Invitation
Design Firm: Joseph Rattan Design, Dallas, Texas, USA
Art Director: Joe Rattan
Designer: Greg Morgan
Client: Dallas Opera Guild

A *Melody* ⊕F DELIGH+

DANCES ⊕N +HE LIPS

WHERE A S⊕NG

AWAI+S I+S RELEASE

LE+ +HE *Wine*

BRING IN +HE PEACE

AND +HE S⊕NG

⊕UR J⊕Y

AS A *Taste* S⊕ SWEE+,

AND A HARM⊕NY

⊕F SUMP+U⊕US ENDEAV⊕R

SHALL +RULY LIF+

+HINE *Heart*

VINTAGE
DALLAS

FRIDAY EVENING
THE
25TH OF MARCH
1994
REGENCY BALLROOM
IN THE FAIRMONT HOTEL
Ross & Akard

ALC 12% TO 15% BY VOL 825 ML

6:30 PM ★ CHAMPAGNE RECEPTION & SILENT AUCTION

BON APPÉTIT

Let the Gala Begin

White
Tablecloth   Elegant
Candlelight

1994

8:00 PM ★ DINNER FOLLOWED BY LIVE AUCTION

Vintage Dallas is an annual wine auction to benefit The Dallas Opera, hosted by The Dallas Opera Guild. Area wine connoisseurs participate in a dignified evening of silent and live auctions, dinner, and wine tasting. In designing this outstanding invitation, Joseph Rattan Design chose to convey the typographic information through the art of wine labels and bottle ephemera. The evident beauty of the labels and the typography that adorns them provided an opportunity to design five original labels to incorporate the invitation information and make the entire concept more memorable. The Vintage Dallas logo, which was provided with the project, has "seal-like" characteristics, so, as a secondary theme, the studio also used wine seals and ephemera motifs that commonly appear on packaging, crates, corks, and the labels themselves. To stay within a limited budget and maintain the elegant tone of the gala, Joseph Rattan Design elected to use three colors and a subdued palette of metallic inks.

EDITOR'S CHOICE

1·2&3

COLOR

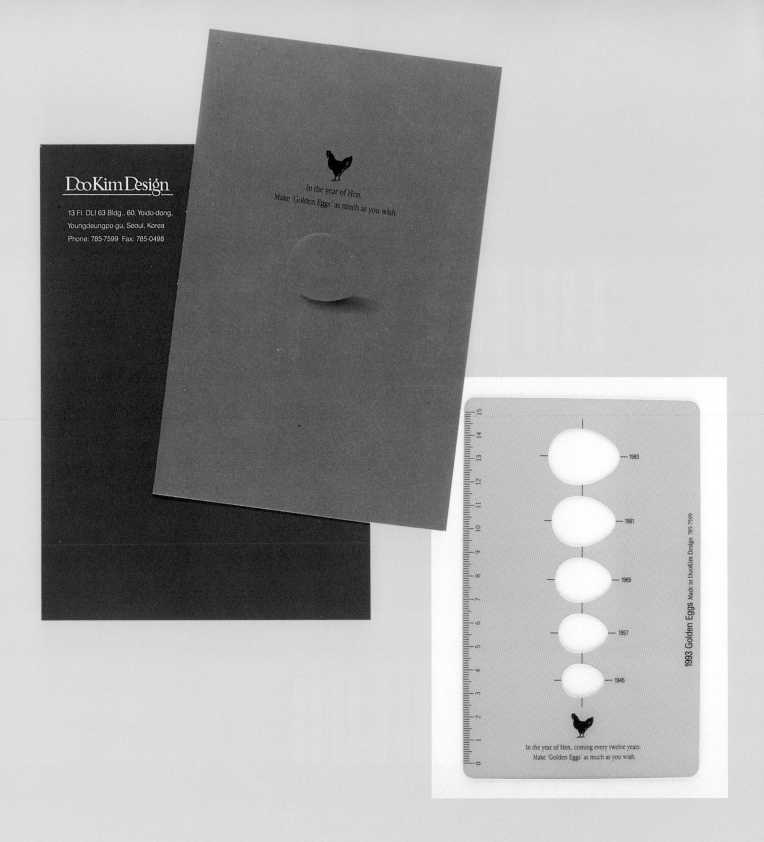

Title: Greeting Card '93
Design Firm: Dookim Design, Seoul, Korea
Art Director: Doo H. Kim
Designers: Dongil Lee, Jiwon Shin
Client: Dookim Design

A gold, egg-shaped sticker is the final touch to a one-color project that — with its glittery selection of shades — results in a glamorous and regal holiday greeting card that reflects well on the sender. 1992 was the year of the hen, and the card — for which a special template was created — expresses the studio's wish for richness and peace in the coming year.

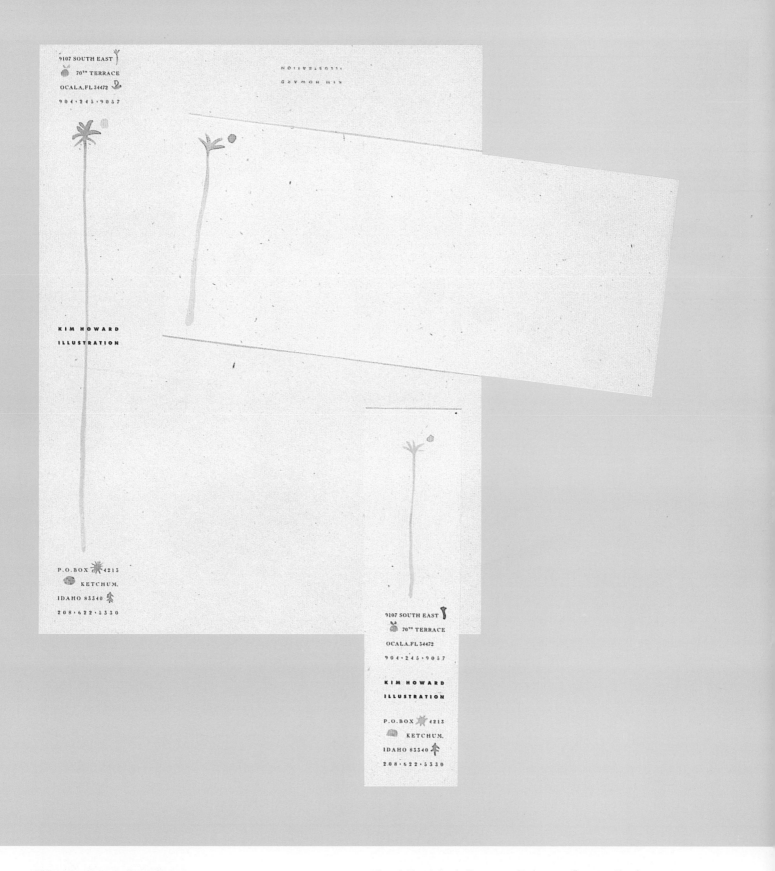

Title: Kim Howard Stationery
Design Firm: Sackett Design Associates,
San Francisco, California, USA
Art Director: Mark Sackett
Designer: Mark Sackett
Client: Kim Howard Illustration

This children's book illustrator splits her time between Florida and Idaho, and had a limited budget for stationery that she used only occasionally. So the papers were designed to accomodate her customized watercolor icons — potatoes, trees, and fruit — hand-painted on each sheet, bookmark, or business card before it's given away. The personal touch takes only a few minutes, and gives the stationery its life and innocence while ensuring both office addresses are well respresented.

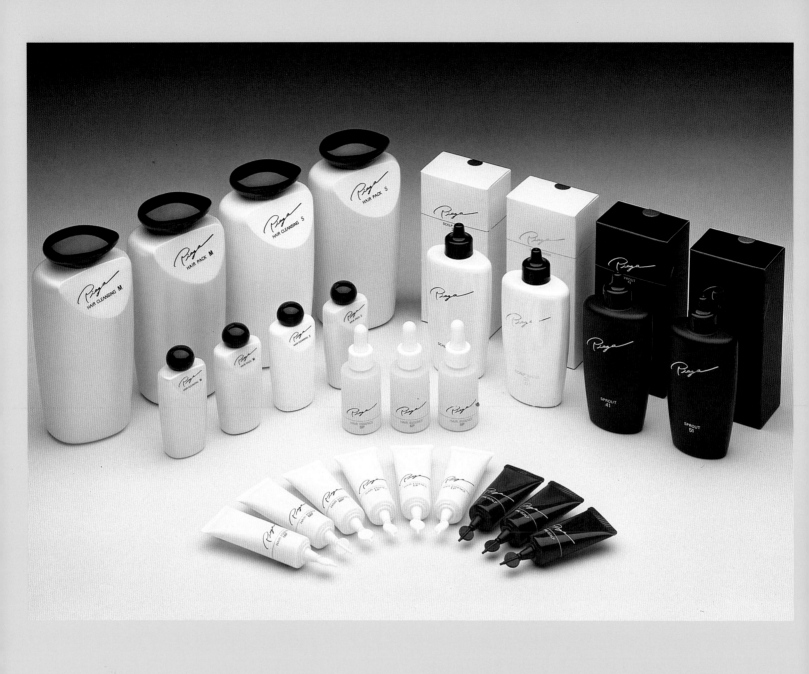

Title: Pieza Series Packaging
Design Firm: Able Design Planning Co., Ltd., Tokyo, Japan
Art Director: Kenji Hanamura
Designer: Motoe Shigeta
Client: Piacelabo Corp.

A tasteful and artistic collection of product packaging for upscale beauty salons, it uses only one color and a graceful, unique assortment of container shapes to make a clear statement about the exceptional quality of its contents. The basis of the color scheme — monochrome — matches the elegance of the salon.

1. What is Trudy Cole-Zielanski?
☐ a graphic designer
☐ an educator
☐ all of the above
☐ none of the above

2. Where is TCZ?
☐ Rt 1 Box 362
   Mount Solon, VA 22843
☐ M114 Duke Hall
   James Madison University
   Harrisonburg, VA 22807
☐ all of the above
☐ none of the above

3. How can she be reached?
☐ by phone at 703-568-3488
☐ by phone at 703-350-2011
☐ by e-mail at
   IN%"FAC_TCOLEZIE
   @VAX2.ACS.JMU.EDU"
☐ all of the above
☐ none of the above

Score: _____

Title: Personal Letterhead
Design Firm: Trudy Cole-Zielanski Design,
Mount Solon, Virginia, USA
Art Director: Trudy Cole-Zielanski
Designer: Trudy Cole-Zielanski
Client: Trudy Cole-Zielanski

Interactive stationery — now *that's* original. In this collection of parodies, the designer drew from the everyday things around her, and used colors that would appropriately represent real life. Read between the lines to discover where the designer teaches, her phone number, even her home address. But be careful... you will be graded on your choices.

Title: Party Invitation
Design Firm: Industry, San Francisco, California, USA
Art Director: Jennifer Burke
Designer: Jennifer Burke
Photographer: Jennifer Burke
Client: Patrick Kane

Flamboyant apparel designer Patrick Kane, when asked to express his feelings about his 30th birthday, struck a pose somewhere between the town crier and "The Scream." The invitation mimicked his two-tone ensemble and reinforced the short-lived quality of a birthday by using black ink on newsprint-colored stock.

Title: WOHNFLEX Poster
Design Firm: BBV Prof. M. Baviera, Zurich, Switzerland
Art Director: Michael Baviera
Designer: Michael Baviera
Client: WOHNFLEX Furniture Boutique

Colors support the variations of "dark to light" prevalent in this poster, and also coincide with a restricted budget. The piece demonstrates the fragility and transparency of a new glass lamp collection and announces an exhibition in the artist's design boutique. All three images are posted together — light, medium, and dark densities — and illuminated from behind.

Title: Anderson Reunion Campaign
Design Firm: Sayles Graphic Design, Des Moines, Iowa, USA
Art Director: John Sayles
Designer: John Sayles
Copywriter: Wendy Lyons
Client: Anderson family

Attendees at this midwestern family reunion received a keepsake box customized for each individual, with a leather-bound brochure/itinerary of events inside. Boxes — fabricated from weathered barnboard — featured found objects on their lids, such as a filed barbed wire and rusted vintage tools. The family had owned a ranch in the Rockies, and had had its own live-stock brand — the inspiration for the brochure's branded cover.

Title: Bob Anderson Stationery
Design Firm: Eskind Waddell, Toronto, Ontario, Canada
Art Director: Malcolm Waddell
Designer: Nicola Lyon
Client: Bob Anderson Photography Limited

An almost ethereal atmosphere is created with a three-dimensional simulation, diffused light, and careful structuring of hard edges with soft edges. Using one color and evoking the idea of light falling onto a surface, the ambiguous letterform was designed for an established photographer, embracing digital imaging.

Green
356

EDITOR'S CHOICE
1·2&3
COLORS

Process
Red

Title: Catalog and Postcard for Tracy Otsuka Esq. Promotion
Design Firm: Spotted Dog Graphics, San Francisco, California, USA
Art Directors: Susannah Bettag, Angela Camacho
Designer: Susannah Bettag
Client: Tracy Otsuka Esq.

It's called "intelligent couture," and it's realized by artistic collateral pieces that hold fabric samples and perceptive philosophies behind this fashion firm's approach. The duotone look complements a line of neutral-colored blouses, and the swatches add a tactile dimension to the catalog. The square format and lack of brash graphics on the cover also help make the piece stand out amongst many other direct mail pieces while maintaining an expensive feel.

Title: AART Group Business Papers
Design Firm: Sackett Design Associates,
San Francisco, California, USA
Art Director: Mark Sackett
Designer: Mark Sackett
Client: The AART Group, Inc.

Reproductions of masterworks abound in this extraordinary
set of business papers that plays with the "AART" name (in a ver-
tical logo used in tandem with the illustrative logo) and with
recurring elements to create the image for this firm representing
fine artists. The suave picture frame logo conveys the various art
represented with its four different sides (contemporary, classical,
linear, and deco) and intricate illustration. The piece incorporated very soft colors that were light enough to be typed upon.

Title: W H Smith Recycled Pads
Design Firm: Trickett & Webb Ltd, London, England
Designers: Lynn Trickett, Brian Webb
Client: W H Smith

To find repartee and whimsy in everyday items takes profound vision and a willingness to look at old things — or even new old things (i.e., recycled) — in a completely fanciful way. The recycled bicycle is made from "postmarks" from torn corners of envelopes. The designers noted that, clearly, with an envrionmentally friendly product, they didn't want to "waste" colors and chose a green background to set off the white writing paper, reinforcing the "green" message. They then selected bright, cheerful blue to enhance the blue writing paper.

Title: MCMXCIV Calendar
Design Firm: Matlik & Schelenz, Essenheim, Germany
Art Directors: Stefan Matlik, Stefan Schelenz
Designers: Stefan Matlik, Stefan Schelenz
Client: Matlik & Schelenz

It's a calendar unlike any you've ever seen, and featuring its two creators. Its unique use of two colors ensures this is one calendar that won't be thrown out at the year's end. The designers told us their strategy was to create something that "tells about our minds and our sense of humor." They chose the colors because "we like them."

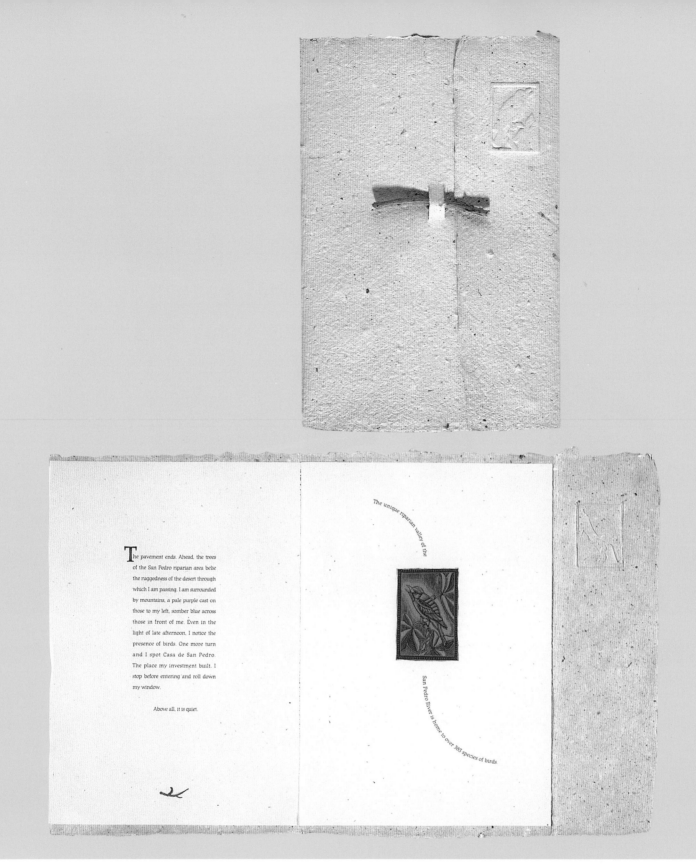

The pavement ends. Ahead, the trees of the San Pedro riparian area belie the ruggedness of the desert through which I am passing. I am surrounded by mountains, a pale purple cast on those to my left, somber blue across those in front of me. Even in the light of late afternoon, I notice the presence of birds. One more turn and I spot Casa de San Pedro. The place my investment built. I stop before entering and roll down my window.

Above all, it is quiet.

The unique riparian valley of the San Pedro River is home to over 385 species of birds.

Title: Casa de San Pedro Promotion
Design Firm: After Hours, Phoenix, Arizona, USA
Art Directors: Russ Haan, Todd Fedell
Designer: Todd Fedell
Illustrator: Bob Case
Client: Casa de San Pedro

As part of a fundraising effort to build an environmentally friendly lodge where guests can relax or participate in ecologically sound endeavors, such as cataloging local plants for research, this piece takes social consciousness a step further. The handsome paper for the brochure (which accompanied a prospectus) is comprised of materials taken from the prospective building site, including dirt and twigs.

24

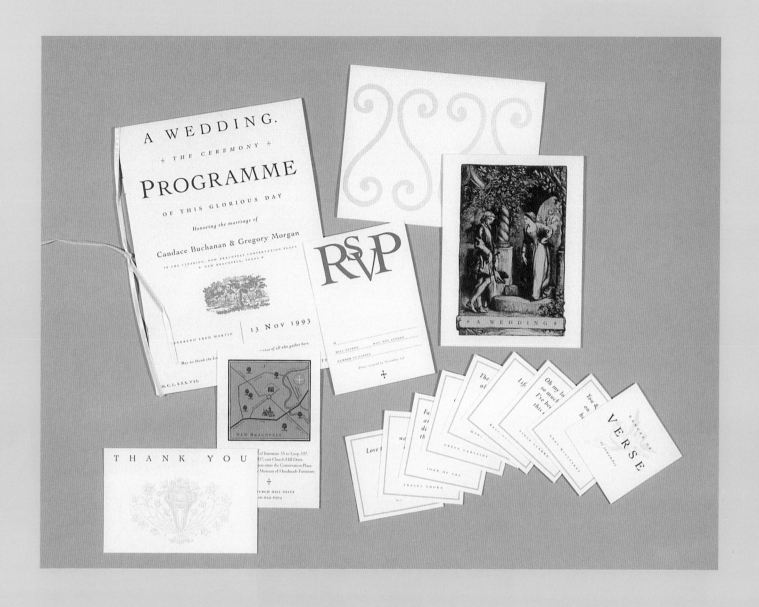

Title: Morgan Wedding Announcement
Design Firms: Joseph Rattan Design, May & Co.,
Dallas, Texas, USA
Art Directors: Greg and Candace Morgan
Designers: Greg and Candace Morgan
Photographers: Greg and Candace Morgan
Client: Greg and Candace Morgan

In accordance with the couple's wishes for a romantic, fabulous celebration, the wedding was arranged in the style of an 18th century, outdoor event. The design conveys the splendor of the day with details that include verse cards of thoughtful and inspired quotes from different songs, which were distributed to guests as a remembrance.

25

our people *our* earth

INTEL'S
ENVIRONMENTAL
RESPONSIBILITY
IN ARIZONA

HOW ARE INTEL EMPLOYEES HELPING TO PREVENT POLLUTION?

WHEN CONSIDERING THE SOURCES OF POLLUTION, MANY PEOPLE THINK OF FACTORIES. BUT POLLUTION COMES FROM MANY SOURCES OTHER THAN MANUFACTURING. FOR EXAMPLE, IN LARGE METROPOLITAN AREAS SUCH AS PHOENIX, 70-80 PERCENT OF TOTAL AIR POLLUTION IS CAUSED BY MOTOR VEHICLE TRAFFIC.

SO IN 1988, INTEL BEGAN A TRAVEL REDUCTION PROGRAM TO HELP CONSERVE FUEL AND KEEP OUR SKIES CLEARER. THIS YEAR, 450 INTEL EMPLOYEES ARE CAR POOLING TO WORK. ANOTHER 150 EMPLOYEES RIDE IN ONE OF OUR 13 VANPOOLS WITH ROUTES THROUGHOUT THE VALLEY. OUR MAIN CAMPUS SHUTTLE BUS SERVICE GIVES A LIFT TO 250 RIDERS EACH WEEK. OUR TWO-WHEEL CROWD INCLUDES 25 BICYCLE COMMUTERS, WHO ENJOY THE USE OF FREE LOCKERS IN OUR RECREATION CENTER. AND MORE THAN 20 EMPLOYEES USE PHOENIX TRANSIT TO COMMUTE.

THIS YEAR WE ALSO BEGAN A HOTLINE FOR EMPLOYEES INTERESTED IN FINDING ALTERNATIVE MODES OF TRANSPORTATION. WE ESTABLISHED A FLEXIBLE WORK HOURS POLICY TO REDUCE THE NUMBER OF EMPLOYEES WHO COMMUTE DURING RUSH HOUR. AND MORE EMPLOYEES THAN EVER ARE WORKING AT HOME, "TELECOMMUTING" WITH COMPUTERS, MODEMS AND PHONES.

ALL LIFE GENERATES WASTE. BUT BY COMBINING OUR IDEAS AND EFFORTS IN SEVERAL AREAS, WE CAN SUBSTANTIALLY REDUCE THE WASTE WE CREATE AND THE NATURAL RESOURCES WE USE. BY WORKING TOGETHER, WE CAN AND DO MAKE A DIFFERENCE.

WHAT ABOUT INTEL FACILITIES IN THE FUTURE? WHAT IMPACT WILL THEY HAVE ON THE ENVIRONMENT?

AS CLOSE TO ZERO AS POSSIBLE. ALL FUTURE INTEL WAFER FABRICATION FACILITIES WILL INCORPORATE THE LATEST TECHNOLOGY TO ACHIEVE ENVIRONMENTALLY FRIENDLY DESIGN AND APPROACH OUR LONG-TERM GOAL OF ZERO EMISSIONS. THESE FACILITIES WILL INCLUDE ENVIRONMENTAL FEATURES SUCH AS:

• THE BEST AVAILABLE CONTROL TECHNOLOGY, TO REDUCE AIR EMISSIONS TO THE LOWEST LEVEL POSSIBLE.

• VAULTED, DOUBLE-WALLED (PIPED) CHEMICAL HANDLING AND STORAGE PROCESSES, EQUIPPED WITH AUTOMATED LEAK DETECTION SYSTEMS TO CONSTANTLY MONITOR EQUIPMENT AND ENSURE SAFE OPERATION.

• WATER RECOVERY AND RECYCLING TO REDUCE WATER REQUIREMENTS.

• AN ENERGY EFFICIENT DESIGN THAT REQUIRES LESS ELECTRICITY THAN COMPARABLE STRUCTURES.

• ENVIRONMENTALLY SENSITIVE ARCHITECTURAL DESIGN, SO THAT BUILDINGS BLEND WITH THE SURROUNDING DESERT TERRAIN.

• LANDSCAPING WITH NATIVE PLANTS THAT REQUIRE LITTLE WATER.

Title: Intel's Environmental Responsibility in Arizona Brochure
Design Firm: Vaughn/Wedeen Creative, Albuquerque, New Mexico, USA
Art Director: Steve Wedeen
Designer: Steve Wedeen
Computer Production: Heather Scanlon
Photographer: Sue Bennett
Client: Intel Corporation

Intel wanted a public relations packet to let people know how the company supports the community. The concept combined all their good work into one big brochure, accented by the color of the sky. The brochure showcases simple elegance with outstanding typography treatment. Small touches make a big impact, like the geometric curves that are mirrored in the wheel, the woman's face, and helmet.

Title: Hat Life Brochure
Design Firm: Alex Bonziglia, New York, New York, USA
Art Director: Alex Bonziglia
Designer: Alex Bonziglia
Photographer: Scott Wipperman
Client: Hat Life

The headwear industry is enjoying a rebirth. In the effort to revitalize an industry clearinghouse, this promotion was developed to supplement a directory. Although the client was quite flexible about the final result, the designer was challenged by a very low budget, so the project used few colors and donated hats to keep costs modest. The concept ensured all images related to the copy.

Title: Annual Report to Donors 1992
Design Firm: Vaughn/Wedeen Creative,
Albuquerque, New Mexico, USA
Art Director: Steve Wedeen
Designer: Steve Wedeen
Photographers: Valerie Santagto, Michael Barley
Client: Southwest Community Health Services

This report presents financial information and also shows appreciation for major supporters. To convey facts and tell the stories of some special people, full sheets were used for one set of text and "sidebar" half-sheets for another. Colors were chosen for class, richness, and honesty. The unassuming cover opens to reveal imaginative spreads that address the sensitivity of its contents as well as the ability of its audience to appreciate inventiveness.

EDITOR'S CHOICE

1·2&3

COLORS

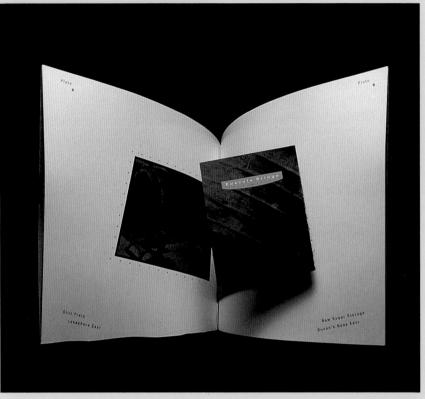

Title: Gill Alkin Photography Brochure
Design Firm: Applied DesignWorks,
Markham, Ontario, Canada
Art Director: David Shelly
Designer: David Shelly
Client: Gill Alkin Photography

Here is a brochure for a still-life photographer with images that will rouse the emptiest soul. In its "booklet-within-a-booklet," the same scene is photographed at varying times of day to display the dissonant affects of light. It provided an element of surprise to the project, with a strip of stock tucked neatly into the leftover space in the larger sheet. The grains and metallic bronze colors were those evident in Toronto's Port Industrial area, where the photos were shot, and the brochure itself has the shape of a ship's hull.

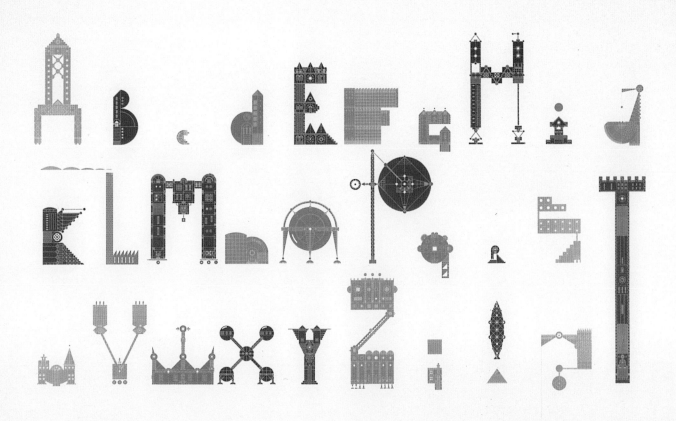

architects language

Title: Architects' Language Poster
Design Firm: Peter Grundy Ownworks, London, England
Designer: Peter Grundy
Client: Peter Grundy

This represents the first of a trilogy of posters based on the designer's concept of decorative letterforms and his illustration of subjects of interest to architects. Colors echo the steel and cement and rust hues of a construction site.

Title: Solo Studio Stationery
Design Firm: Pepellashi & Rae, Southfield, Michigan, USA
Art Directors: John Latin, Bernie Solo
Designer: John Latin
Client: Bernie Solo

This stationery was designed for an illustrator/craftsman who creates limited edition lamps — hence the light bulb motif. There isn't a boring side to any piece — envelopes are enhanced with photos, stationery and cards with type treatments, and all are dipped, front and back, in rich colors. The intention was something bold and graphic in a workingman, "Detroit" style. The stock is a newer brand of butcher's paper, with an overall dull appearance and scattered glossy areas, so that, when printed, some ink appears dull, while some doesn't look fully dry.

Title: Univel Overview Brochure
Design Firm: Mortensen Design,
Mountain View, California, USA
Art Director: Gordon Mortensen
Designer: Gordon Mortensen
Illustrator: Chris Gall
Client: Univel

Technology presented with intelligence — that's the result of upfront illustrations and design constructed with insight and originality on every page. To make the brochure dramatic and memorable, red, black, and yellow were used, as they are perceived as powerful colors. The "textured" stock was a bonus, as it worked like an extra color and had a tactile illusion to it. The customers of this networking firm were represented in the icons.

Title: **Little Angel Music Centre Business Papers**
Design Firm: Cat Lam Design Co., Tai Po, Hong Kong
Art Director: Catherine Lam Siu Hung
Designer: Catherine Lam Siu Hung
Client: Little Angel Music Centre

Light and lyrical in color, layout, and placement of information on the page, these print pieces are almost gossamer. Their airy feel lends charm to invoices and letterhead alike. Even the typography is buoyant, and supported by carefully muted colors and symbols appropriate for the client represented — musical notes, a metronome, piano keys.

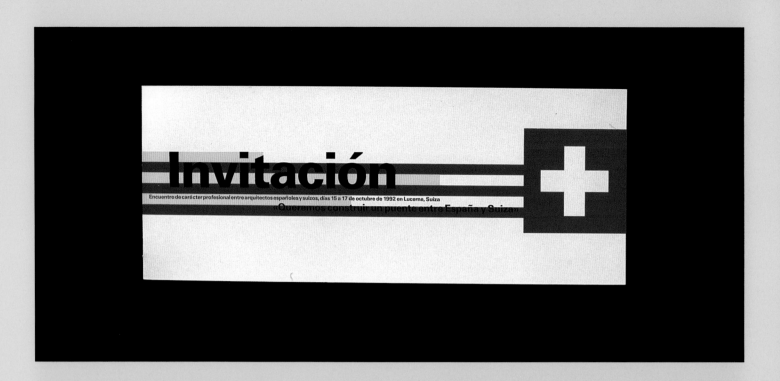

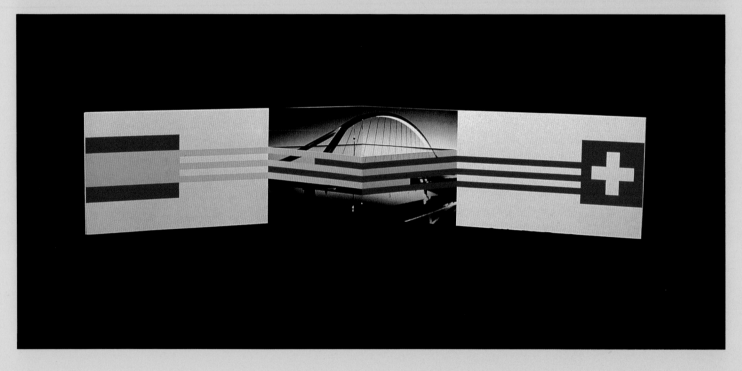

Title: Invitation to an Architect's Meeting
Design Firm: Wolf Henkel CI-Studio, Luzern, Switzerland
Art Director: Wolf Henkel
Designers: Wolf Henkel, Walter Invernizzi
Client: Schindler Management AG, Ebikon/Luzern

Bright colors add festivity to this invitation from the world's second-largest manufacturer of elevators to renowned Spanish architects to a meeting with their Swiss counterparts. The inivtation's white cross on a red background connotes the Swiss flag, and the yellow and red motif represents the Spanish flag. The three yellow and red stripes — part of the Schindler logo — join as a symbol of friendship.

MERIT
1·2&3
COLOR

Brown
471

Title: Romeo and Juliet Poster
Design Firm: Sommese Design, State College, Pennsylvania, USA
Art Director: Lanny Sommese
Designer: Lanny Sommese
Client: Pennsylvania State University

A single-color design and creative contours transform this age-old tale into drama and nuance. The simplicity of the carefully structured work belies its subtleties, where a heart and a dagger can be found in a kiss.

Title: Buckhead Nursery Packaging
Design Firm: Lyerly Peniston Design, Atlanta, Georgia, USA
Designer & Illustrator: Lyerly Peniston
Client: Buckhead Nursery

These imaginative seed packets and the flower bulb container project an earth-friendly theme; all were produced of completely recycled materials — including the string (made of recycled paper) and the twig.

39

Title: etaoin shrdlu Book
Design Firm: University of Illinois at Urbana-Champaign, Champaign, Illinois, USA
Art Director: Nan Goggin
Designers: Graduate students of Graphic Design
Client: University of Illinois

A tightly crafted edition limited to 150, this piece is called a "collaborative endeavor in book design," where innovative graphic techniques are enlivened with quotes from a variety of individuals from C.G. Jung to Emily Dickinson.

North Carolina Literary Review

NC
LR.

A. R. Ammons

Linda Beatrice Brown

Fred Chappell

Janet Lembke

—

A Special Feature

—

John Lawson
and the Tuscarora

—

summer 1992

Title: North Carolina Literary Review Book Cover
Design Firm: East Carolina University School of Art,
Greenville, North Carolina, USA
Art Director: Eva Roberts
Designers: Eva Roberts, Stanton Blakeslee
Editor: Alex Albright
Client: ECU English Department

ECU's School of Art found a budget-conscious way to create
interest in its poetry, essays, and other writing with a refined
approach and a single color. Its color choice communicates
a sedate tone while clearly featuring the highlights inside.

Title: Wedding Invitation
Design Firm: John Evans Design, Dallas, Texas, USA
Art Director: John Evans
Designer: John Evans
Client: Dan Evans and Michelle Vickrey

A whimsical work that makes great use of black and white by building curiosity with a simple cover and playful script. It reveals a celebratory design inside and maintains a sense of ceremony with its attractive choice of type.

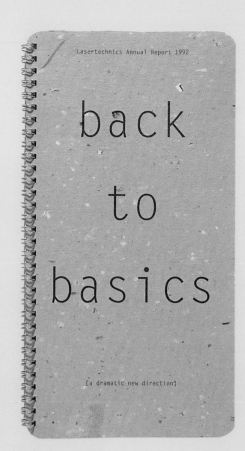

Lasertechnics Annual Report 1992

back
to
basics

[a dramatic new direction]

our
future
begins
now.

[Although we will always watch for
new opportunities, our future success
starts with our efforts today.]

[TEN]

A second reason to be optimistic about our Laser Marking Division is the positive response we have received to Xymark, a new coding laser that we are exclusively marketing in the United States for Coherent Hull, Ltd., its British manufacturer. Simply put, Xymark combines all the advantages of ink jet coders – simplicity, versatility, flexibility – with all the advantages of lasers: it's a clean, safe, economical, environmentally friendly coder that leaves permanent marks.

These two factors – the Blazer™ 6000's possible entry into the beverage industry, and the new Xymark – lead us to expect a steady increase in Laser Marking Division sales and profit potential over the next two years. These are existing products in a field where Lasertechnics enjoys an excellent reputation.

Our optimism reflects a new focus on real products with current markets. In the past, our attention to ancillary or speculative businesses and products diluted our employees' efforts. That won't happen anymore. Some of the finest people in the laser industry work here at Lasertechnics. They have made major contributions to our company, and we thank them and our management team for their dedication during

[ELEVEN]

Title: Lasertechnics Annual Report
Design Firm: Vaughn/Wedeen Creative, Albuquerque, New Mexico, USA
Art Director: Steve Wedeen
Designer: Steve Wedeen
Writer & Computer Production: Nathan James
Client: Lasertechnics, Inc.

The theme "back to basics" is echoed in all facets of this unique annual report, from its unprententious color choice to its easy-to-read typeface to its direct and concise manner of information dissemination.

43

Title: Mahlum & Nordfors Flip Book
Design Firm: Hornall Anderson Design Works,
Seattle, Washington, USA
Art Director: Jack Anderson
Designers: Jack Anderson, Leo Raymundo
Client: Mahlum & Nordfors McKinley Gordon

Is the opposite of logic always imagination? It is in this highly original work that animates symbols that are "grounded in discipline" until they are animated by passion. Use of just one color concentrates the reader's eye on the action.

Title: Nexo Stationery Package
Design Firm: Visual Asylum, San Diego, California, USA
Art Directors: MaeLin Levine and Amy Jo Levine
Designer: Christine Daschner
Client: Viniul International

Combine white with black, rule with curve, and set it on a page or a business card and you have the bold, aggressive print products for a progressive California company. The two-sided business cards display critical information while showcasing a powerful logo.

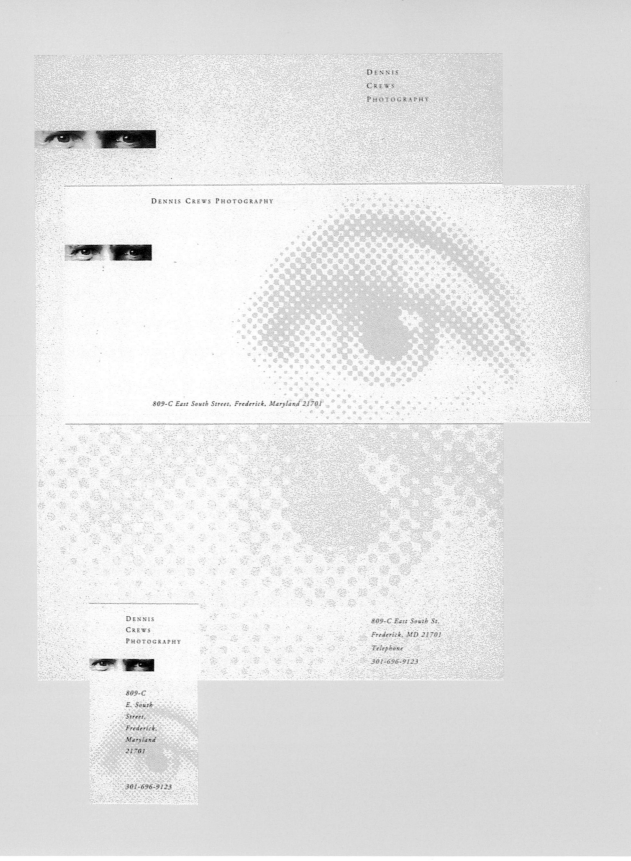

Title: Dennis Crews Stationery
Design Firm: Dever Designs, Inc., Laurel, Maryland, USA
Art Director: Jeffrey L. Dever
Designer: Jeffrey L. Dever
Photographer: Dennis Crews
Client: Dennis Crews Photography

If someone is watching you, you'd probably prefer the expressive eyes that grace this effective design in both photograph and image, communicating a sense of humor as well as a respect for the beauty and art of vision.

Title: The Bachelors and Spinsters Ball 1994 Calendar
Design Firm: Burton Nesbitt Graphic Design,
Adelaide, South Australia, Australia
Art Director: Burton Nesbitt Graphic Design
Designer: Burton Nesbitt Graphic Design
Printer: Finsbury Press
Client: B & S Ball Publications

A collection of offbeat photos, unconventional wisdom, and folklore in verse, this calendar celebrates and archives the memories of the event. It also acts as a fundraising device for the Royal Flying Doctor Services, providing rural Australians with aerial health services.

Osamu Kuninaka
EXECUTIVE CHEF

Tel: 941-9222
#201-2764 Barnet Hwy.
Coquitlam, British Columbia
V3E 1B9

Tel: 941-9222
#201-2764 Barnet Hwy.
Coquitlam, British Columbia
V3E 1B9

Title: Osamu Sushi Stationery
Design Firm: Profile Design,
Vancouver, British Columbia, Canada
Designer: Linda Mitsui
Client: Osamu Sushi

Seafoam green is an inspired color to depict a sushi bar, and the sheet specked with black lends an interesting background perspective to a logo that artistically expresses the restaurant's specialty.

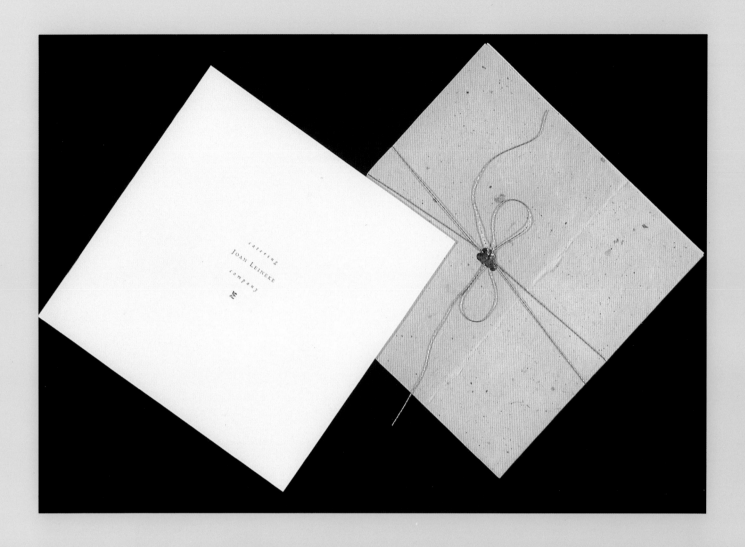

Title: Joan Leineke Catering Brochure
Design Firm: The Dunlavey Studio, Inc.,
Sacramento, California, USA
Art Director: Michael Dunlavey
Designer: Kevin Yee
Client: Joan Leineke

A bit of gold braid tied and held in place with sealing wax
offers an additional elegant touch to the fragile paper sleeve
that holds sample menus from an upscale catering firm.

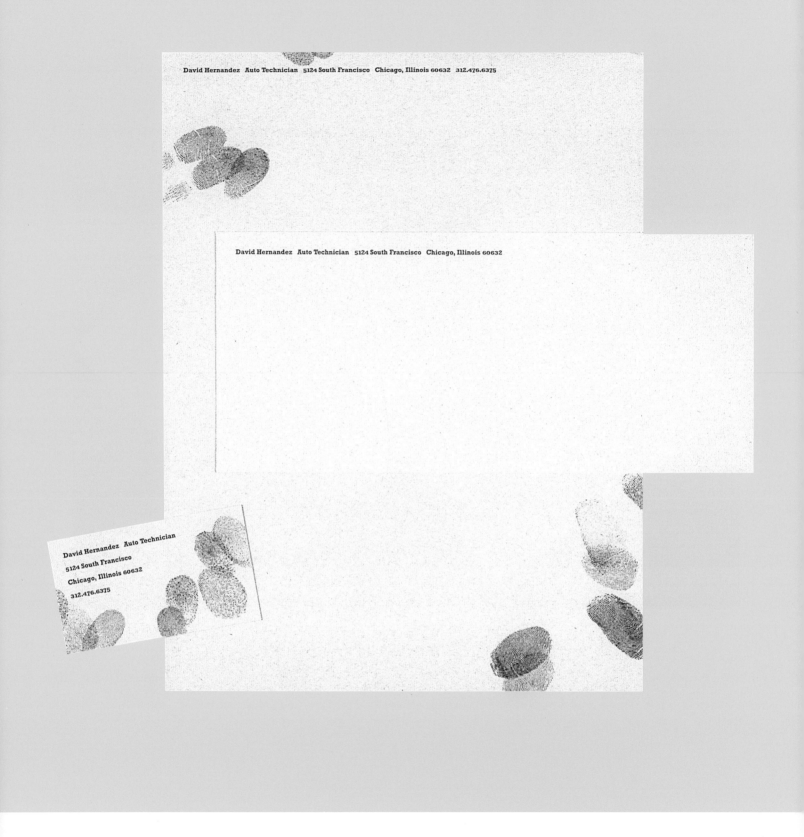

Title: Mechanic Stationery
Design Firm: SullivanPerkins, Dallas, Texas, USA
Art Director: Art Garcia
Designer: Art Garcia
Client: David Hernandez

Scattered fingerprints lend a playful tone to the stationery of an auto technician, and the color choice becomes another appropriate element — the undeniable hue of oil, grime, hard work.

Amy and David
have something to declare.

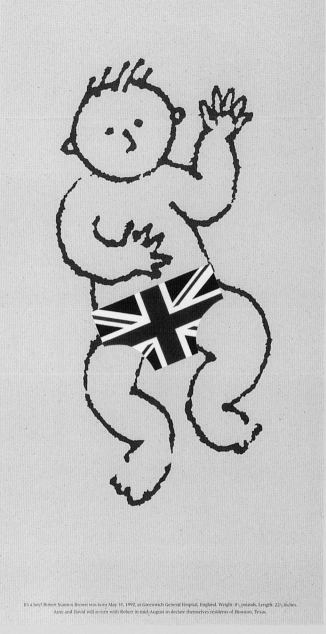

It's a boy! Robert Stanton Brown was born May 31, 1992, at Greenwich General Hospital, England. Weight: 8½ pounds. Length: 22½ inches.
Amy and David will return with Robert in mid-August to declare themselves residents of Houston, Texas.

Title: Robert Brown Birth Announcement
Design Firm: SullivanPerkins, Dallas, Texas, USA
Art Director: Ron Sullivan
Designer: Rob Wilson
Illustrator: Rob Wilson
Copywriter: Hilary Kennard
Client: Bob Davis

An ingenious use of a single color, comprising an official-looking document with a surprise inside. The infant within is clad in a color reproduction of the flag indicating his country of birth.

Title: Image Package Business Papers
Design Firm: Beauchamp Design, San Diego, California, USA
Art Director: Michele Beauchamp
Designer: Michele Beauchamp
Client: Beauchamp Design

The initial "B" and subtle coloring produced at different percentages combine to make these print pieces look professional, while customizing them with a sense of warmth and femininity.

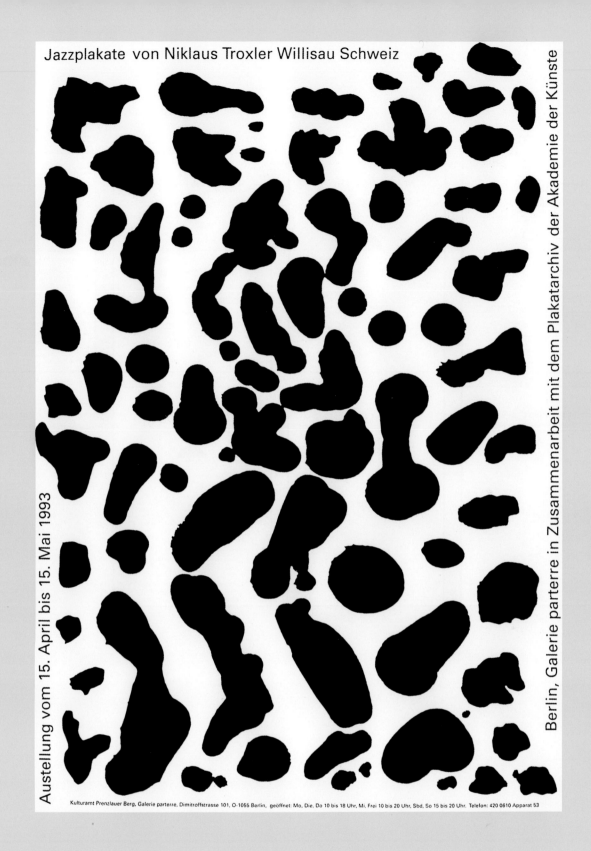

Jazzplakate von Niklaus Troxler Willisau Schweiz

Berlin, Galerie parterre in Zusammenarbeit mit dem Plakatarchiv der Akademie der Künste

Austellung vom 15. April bis 15. Mai 1993

Kulturamt Prenzlauer Berg, Galerie parterre, Dimitroffstrasse 101, O-1055 Berlin, geöffnet: Mo, Die, Do 10 bis 18 Uhr, Mi, Frei 10 bis 20 Uhr, Sbd, So 15 bis 20 Uhr. Telefon: 420 0610 Apparat 53

Title: Jazz Poster of Niklaus Troxler
Design Firm: Niklaus Troxler Design Studio,
Willisau, Switzerland
Art Director: Niklaus Troxler
Designer: Niklaus Troxler
Client: Akademie der Künste Berlin

The energy and excitement of jazz is actively projected in this high-voltage poster that relies only on black and white to get its point across, and succeeds without question.

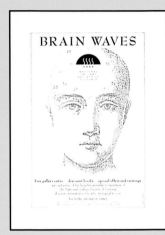

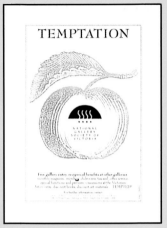

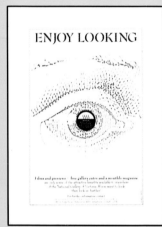

Title: NGSV Advertising Campaign
Design Firm: Mammoliti Chan Design,
West Brunswick, Victoria, Australia
Art Director: Tony Mammoliti
Designer: Tony Mammoliti
Client: National Gallery Society of Australia

Although these campaign elements are joined by similar head-
lines and illustrative styles, the disparity of their focus, describing
a multitude of gallery services, provides a thoughtful theme and
creates cordial requests for membership.

Title: You'll Flip For This Event Promotion
Design Firm: Sayles Graphic Design, Des Moines, Iowa, USA
Art Director: John Sayles
Designer: John Sayles
Copywriter: Wendy Lyons
Client: Boys and Girls Club

A clever container housing a utensil and coupons uses different papers to create its vivid, multi-hued image, but in actuality, remains committed to a one-color design.

Title: Fix It Now Or Fix It Later Poster
Design Firm: Trudy Cole-Zielanski Design,
Mount Solon, Virginia, USA
Art Director: Trudy Cole-Zielanski
Designer: Trudy Cole-Zielanski
Client: Animal Welfare

Underneath the stark paint of this poster is a softhearted message to help control the population of unwanted animals. It is an authentic one-color piece, achieved with a split fountain technique and two colors, but with a single screenprint.

Purple
2514

MERIT
1·2&3
COLORS

Green
3355

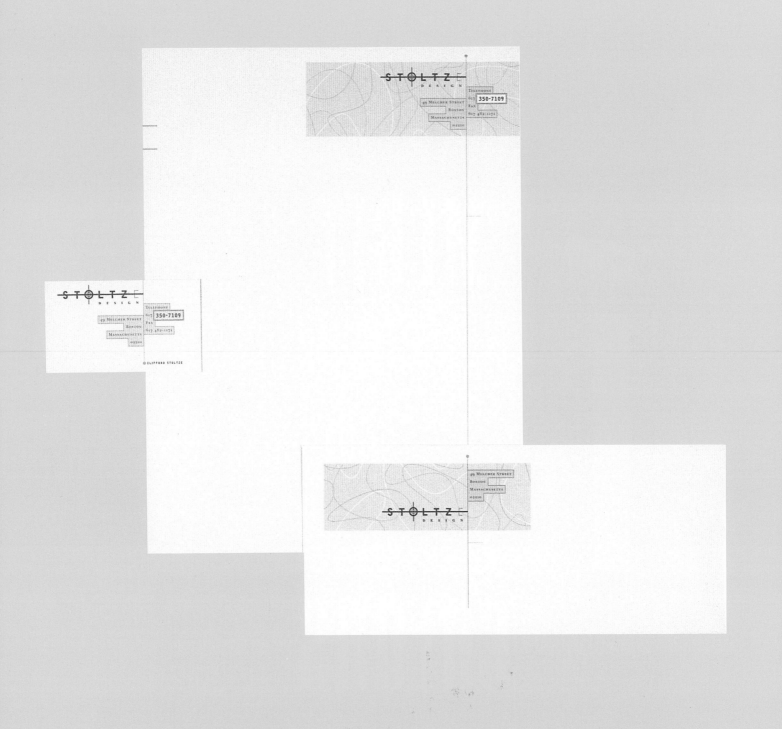

Title: Stoltze Design Letterhead
Design Firm: Stoltze Design, Boston, Massachusetts, USA
Art Director: Clifford Stoltze
Designer: Clifford Stoltze
Client: Stoltze Design

The traditional business tone of most stationery is made unique and progressive by the addition of original graphic elements and subtle color choices.

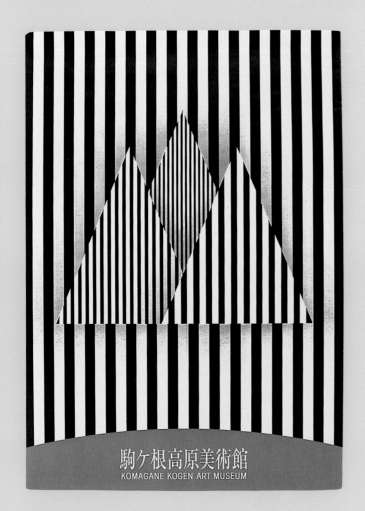

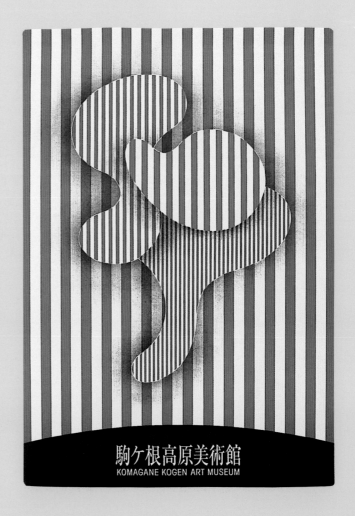

Title: Komagane Kogen Art Museum Campaign
Design Firm: Hiromura Design Office, Tokyo, Japan
Art Director: Massaki Hiromura
Designers: Massaki Hiromura, Nobuhiko Aizawa
Client: Komagane Kogen Art Museum

Bold, geometric shapes are layered onto powerful backgrounds that make excellent use of black and white as well as commanding colors in this group of posters promoting museum events.

59

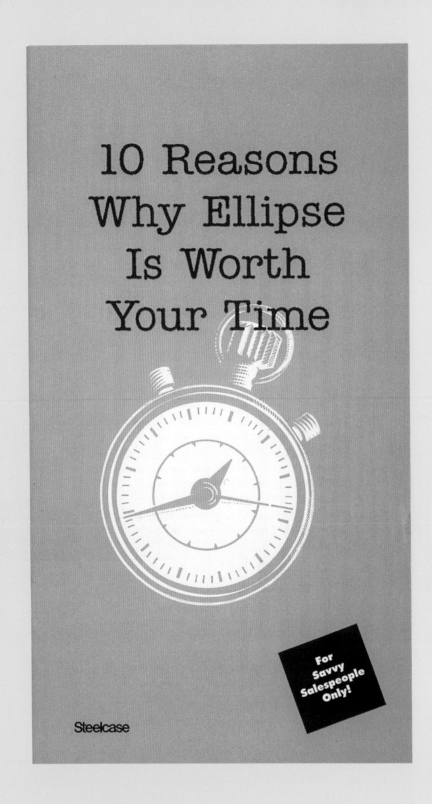

Title: Ellipse Sales Guide - 10 Reasons
Design Firm: Agnew Moyer Smith Inc.,
Pittsburgh, Pennsylvania, USA
Art Director: Don Moyer
Designer: Gina Kennedy
Client: Steelcase Inc.

Blaze orange is eye-catching as well as an appropriate background color on which to set black type. Unpretentious illustrations add appeal to the print piece.

Title: Design Metro Stationery
Design Firm: Design Metro, Portland, Oregon, USA
Art Director: Sara Ledgard Rogers
Designers: Julie Cristeno, Sara Rogers
Photographer: Christine Cody
Client: Design Metro

Hard and soft images, imagination vs. reality, or, as the business card states, "graphic + product = design." Here, dissimilar replicas are linked in a wholly fascinating way.

61

Title: Presents of Mind Stoltze Design Holiday Cards
Design Firm: Stoltze Design, Boston, Massachusetts, USA
Art Director: Clifford Stoltze
Designers: Clifford Stoltze, Peter Farrell, Rebecca Fagan
Client: Stoltze Design

A joyful collection of holiday cards, each with a wish that may bring love, peace, and understanding to the recipient. Colors are subtle and lend sincerity to the message.

Title: **Betty the Yeti Poster**
Design Firm: Modern Dog, Seattle, Washington, USA
Art Director: Michael Strassburger
Designer: Michael Strassburger
Illustrator: Michael Strassburger
Client: Act Theater

Potential audiences are lured by the droll portrayal of a fictitious creature, which is enlivened by a curious illustration and spare use of color.

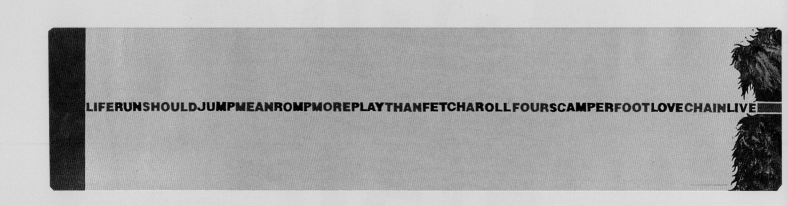

Title: Man's Best Friend Poster
Design Firm: Trudy Cole-Zielanski Design,
Mount Solon, Virginia, USA
Art Director: Trudy Cole-Zielanski
Designer: Trudy Cole-Zielanski
Client: Animal Welfare

Sometimes so much can be read into so little, like a few
well-placed words that draw the eye horizontally to a thought-
provoking message at the end.

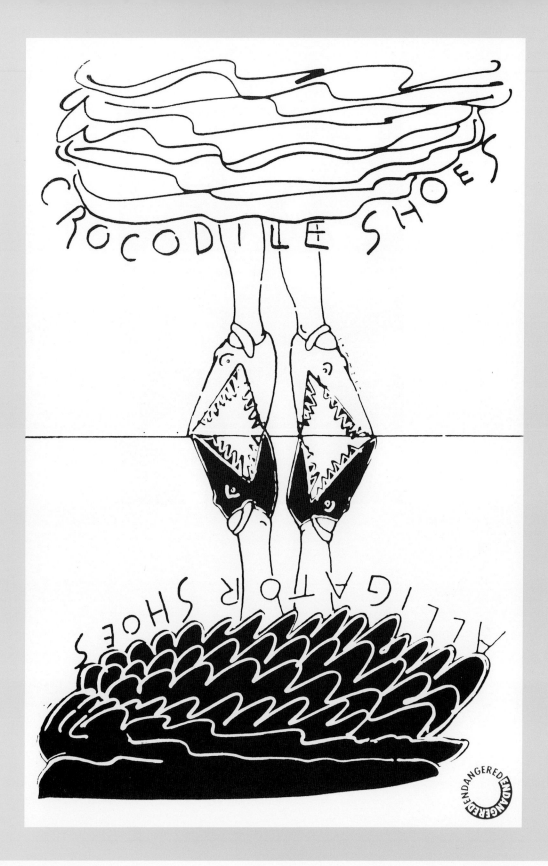

Title: Endangered Alligator Shoes Poster
Design Firm: Sommese Design,
State College, Pennsylvania, USA
Art Director: Lanny Sommese
Designer: Lanny Sommese
Client: Pennsylvania State University Institute for Arts and
Humanistic Studies

Shoes metamorphosize into both toothy creatures and
statements for the issue of preservation, while the tiny red
stamp in the corner draws the focus.

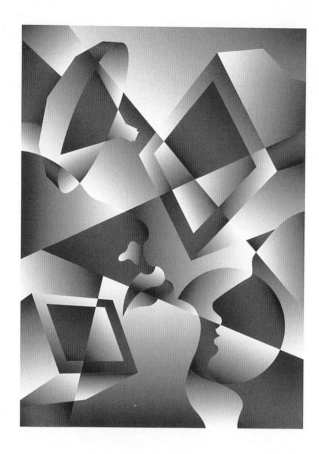

"WE'RE CHANGING

THE WAY YOU VIEW

TECHNOLOGY"

•

PREMIERING

OCTOBER 6, 1993

Title: Novell Television Poster
Design Firm: Huddleston Malone Design Inc.,
Salt Lake City, Utah, USA
Art Directors: Dave Malone, Gail Pierce Watne
Designer: Dave Malone
Illustrators: Dave Malone, Kirk Rawlins
Client: Novell

A poster to promote the introduction of a new television network features an intense design that seems to introduce another light source as well as a third dimension.

Title: Autobahn Clothing Tag
Design Firm: Dookim Design, Seoul, Korea
Art Director: Doo H. Kim
Designers: Dongil Lee, Ji-Won Shin
Client: Non-No Inc./Autobahn

An uncommon concept results in "German military look" casual clothing that appeals to young adult consumers. The "bullet holes" design element is used in many of the fashion's applications.

2 WORLD WARS

80 RELIGIONS

188 COUNTRIES

6,000 LANGUAGES

15,700,905 BOOKS

ONE HUMANITY

OUR COMPLEX WORLD:
BALANCING UNITY & DIVERSITY

Honors Forum Lecture Series September 29, 1993 - April 20, 1994

Title: 1993 Honors Poster
Design Firm: After Hours, Phoenix, Arizona, USA
Art Director: Russ Haan
Designer: Todd Fedell
Illustrator: Bob Case
Client: Maricopa Community College District

The copy is tightly associated with the visual depictions of global statistics. The compelling figures — did we know there were 6,000 languages in the world? — are strategically placed for maximum authority.

Title: Light Gear POP Campaign
Design Firm: Mires Design, San Diego, California, USA
Art Director: Scott Mires
Designer: Scott Mires
Illustrator: Tracy Sabin
Client: LA Gear

The client requested a look that was aggressive and hip, and these packaging and point-of-purchase designs work well for a trendy line of illuminated footwear.

Title: Graffiti Newsletter
Design Firm: Barton/Komai, Fountain Valley, California, USA
Art Director: Jeff Barton
Designer: Jeff Barton
Client: Art Direction and Design in Orange County

Red was an inspired choice for this dominant color, as it can indicate vibrance; and this newsletter is certainly not somber or sluggish. Exceptional use of columns and illustration placement add to the effect.

Title: Endangered Indian Python Poster
Design Firm: Sommese Design,
State College, Pennsylvania, USA
Art Director: Lanny Sommese
Designer: Lanny Sommese
Client: Pennsylvania State University Institute for Arts and
Humanistic Studies

It's a circumspect message, but its application is plain.
This piece illustrates not one snake but two by encouraging
the viewer to look closely and observe a modest statement,
boldly put.

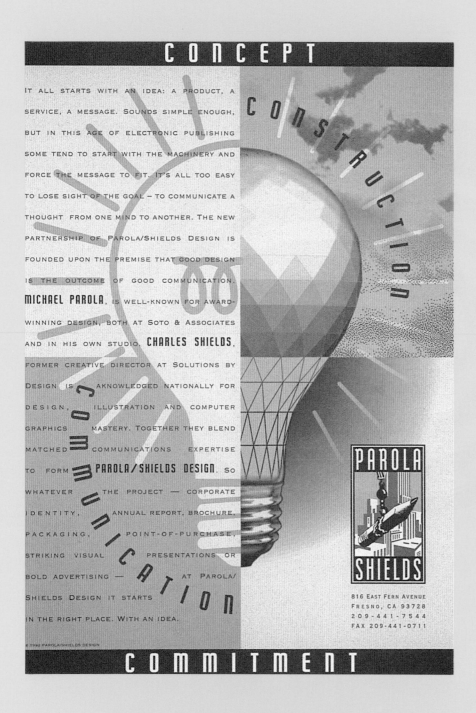

CONCEPT

IT ALL STARTS WITH AN IDEA: A PRODUCT, A SERVICE, A MESSAGE. SOUNDS SIMPLE ENOUGH, BUT IN THIS AGE OF ELECTRONIC PUBLISHING SOME TEND TO START WITH THE MACHINERY AND FORCE THE MESSAGE TO FIT. IT'S ALL TOO EASY TO LOSE SIGHT OF THE GOAL — TO COMMUNICATE A THOUGHT FROM ONE MIND TO ANOTHER. THE NEW PARTNERSHIP OF PAROLA/SHIELDS DESIGN IS FOUNDED UPON THE PREMISE THAT GOOD DESIGN IS THE OUTCOME OF GOOD COMMUNICATION. MICHAEL PAROLA, IS WELL-KNOWN FOR AWARD-WINNING DESIGN, BOTH AT SOTO & ASSOCIATES AND IN HIS OWN STUDIO. CHARLES SHIELDS, FORMER CREATIVE DIRECTOR AT SOLUTIONS BY DESIGN IS ACKNOWLEDGED NATIONALLY FOR DESIGN, ILLUSTRATION AND COMPUTER GRAPHICS MASTERY. TOGETHER THEY BLEND MATCHED COMMUNICATIONS EXPERTISE TO FORM PAROLA/SHIELDS DESIGN. SO WHATEVER THE PROJECT — CORPORATE IDENTITY, ANNUAL REPORT, BROCHURE, PACKAGING, POINT-OF-PURCHASE, STRIKING VISUAL PRESENTATIONS OR BOLD ADVERTISING — AT PAROLA/SHIELDS DESIGN IT STARTS IN THE RIGHT PLACE. WITH AN IDEA.

© 1992 PAROLA/SHIELDS DESIGN

CONSTRUCTION

COMMUNICATION

COMMITMENT

PAROLA SHIELDS

816 EAST FERN AVENUE
FRESNO, CA 93728
209-441-7544
FAX 209-441-0711

Title: **Parola Shields Poster**
Design Firm: Shields Design, Fresno, California, USA
Art Director: Charles Shields
Designer: Charles Shields
Client: Parola Shields Design

How many ways can one illustrate an idea? Here's a self-promotion where color forms an effective backdrop to an interplay of type and graphics that reveals a detailed message from several perspectives.

Title: DSVC Show Invitation '94
Design Firm: Joseph Rattan Design, Dallas, Texas, USA
Art Director: Joe Rattan
Designer: Diana McKnight
Client: Dallas Society of Visual Communicators

Here's an invitation comprised of a harmonious medley
of pieces, all festive, all evoking curiosity about the event
and delivering valuable information about it in a direct
and friendly manner.

The Great Characters -1
1993
Takashi Akiyama

Title: The Great Characters - 1 Book Jacket
Design Firm: Takashi Akiyama Studio, Tokyo, Japan
Designer: Takashi Akiyama
Client: Takashi Akiyama

This book jacket shows the effervescent style of an illustrator who favors creating characters from heavy lines, outlandish perspectives, and sometimes a little color scattered here and there.

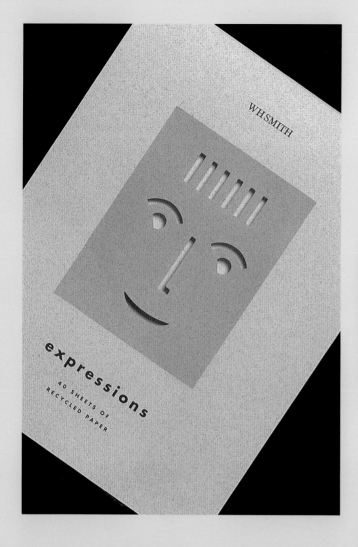

Title: W H Smith Expressions Writing Pads
Design Firm: Trickett & Webb Ltd, London, England
Designers: Lynn Trickett, Brian Webb, Avril Broadly
Client: W H Smith

Attention-getting papers with fanciful expressions successfully mingle a studio's design acumen with a sense of humor. Two colors are chosen with regard for character, and applied inconspicuously.

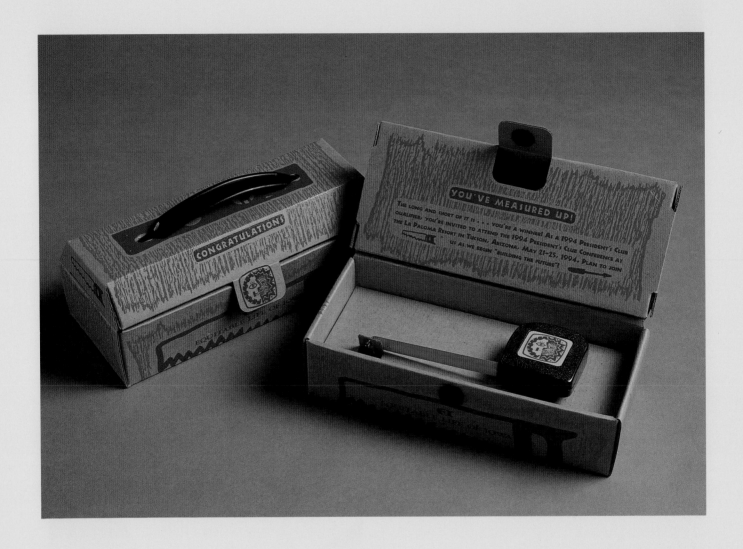

Title: Building the Future
Design Firm: Sayles Graphic Design, Des Moines, Iowa, USA
Art Director: John Sayles
Designer: John Sayles
Client: Equitable

Is it a tool box or just a first-class packaging design? This box, tinged with orange and magenta, houses a ruler with which recipients can ensure they "measure up" to all company standards, and the promotional piece reflects well on the client.

Title: **Who's Fred Poster**
Design Firm: Shields Design, Fresno, California, USA
Art Director: Charles Shields
Designer: Charles Shields
Client: Fresno Graphic Group

Count on designers to come up with a fresh perspective —
on designers. Bright colors underscore this poster's visibility,
and creative copy sustains an imaginative theme where social
encounters become opportunities for both networking and
some old-fashioned, meaningful conversation.

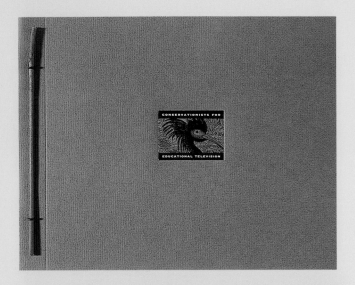

This statement is as true today as ever. Unfortunately for most of us in the general public, it's the other side of the conservation story that we often don't hear. Without this information, we would have never known that fishermen caught more salmon in Prince William Sound a year after the

ANY STORY SOUNDS TRUE

Valdez oil spill than before, or that there are more trees today in the United States than there were

UNTIL SOMEONE TELLS THE

100 years ago, or that hunters, through licenses, duck stamps and excise taxes on equipment and

OTHER SIDE AND SETS

ammunition, are the primary revenue source for managing wildlife – to date more than $12 billion!

THE RECORD STRAIGHT.

Conservationists for Educational Television (CETV) is a non-profit organization founded in 1991,

PROVERBS 18:17

dedicated to making sure the general public has adequate information on conservation issues so wise decisions can be made. The issues are too important not to have this information. Conservation and management of fish, wildlife, forests, agriculture/ranch lands, minerals and fossil fuels are not about saving the world, they are about ensuring our future.

Title: CETV Brochure
Design Firm: SullivanPerkins, Dallas, Texas, USA
Art Directors: Ron Sullivan, Dan Richards
Designer: Dan Richards
Client: Conservationists for Educational Television

Warmly textured cover stock, recycled paper, and down-to-earth elements — animals, fish, and birds illustrated throughout — result in a brochure which goes beyond the standard "green" theme into something approaching fine art.

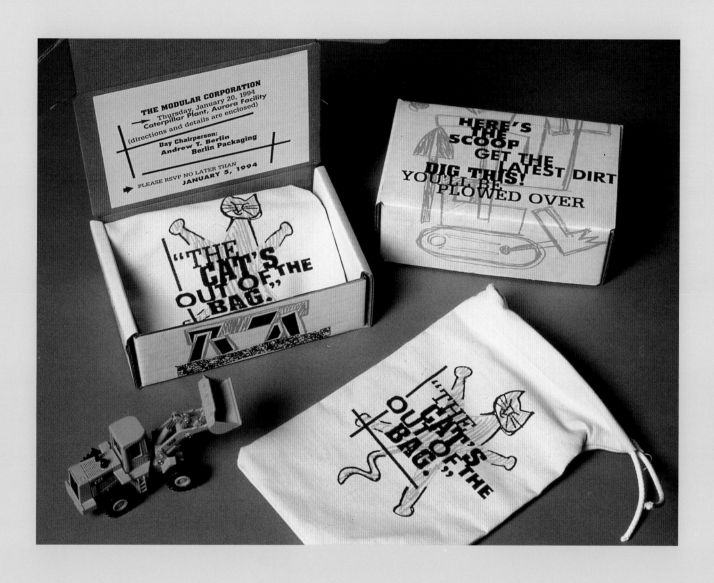

Title: The Cat's Out of the Bag Promotion
Design Firm: Sayles Graphic Design, Des Moines, Iowa, USA
Art Director: John Sayles
Designer: John Sayles
Copywriter: Andrew Berlin
Client: Berlin Packaging

To produce a playful promotion without compromising the message, this design used simplicity, wit, and a lot of repartee. Color becomes an important element that unifies the several pieces.

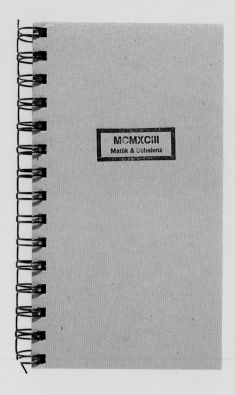

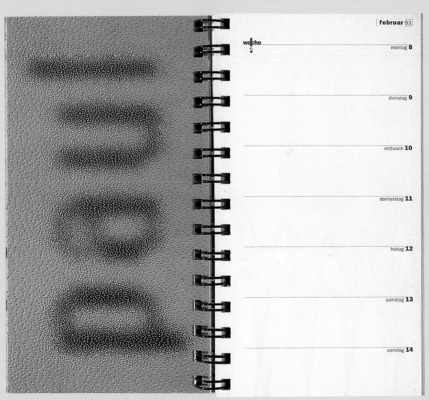

Title: MCMXCIII
Design Firm: Matlik & Schelenz, Essenheim, Germany
Art Directors: Stefan Matlik, Stefan Schelenz
Designers: Stefan Matlik, Stefan Schelenz
Client: Matlik & Schelenz

An appointment book crowded with imaginative works of art and photography, this piece surely made each week a new experience in the fascinating and the extreme.

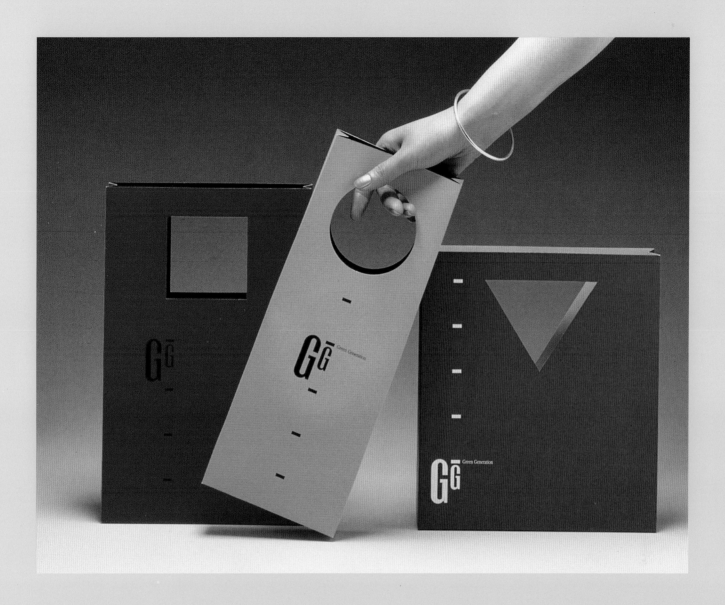

Title: Shopping Bags
Design Firm: Dookim Design, Seoul, Korea
Art Director: Doo H. Kim
Designers: Dongil Lee, Ji-Won Shin
Client: Pacific Corporation/G.G. Cosmetics

Die-cut handles replace the more common non-biodegradable materials. The bags' primary colors reinforce the idea of youth and freshness for a cosmetics line catering to teens.

**Title: National Community College Chair
Academy Stationery**
Design Firm: After Hours, Phoenix, Arizona, USA
Art Director: Russ Haan
Designer: Brad Smith
Photography: Art Holeman
Client: National Community College Chair Academy

An exceptional example of few colors and fascinating photography working hard to create an illusion of space, movement, and sophistication.

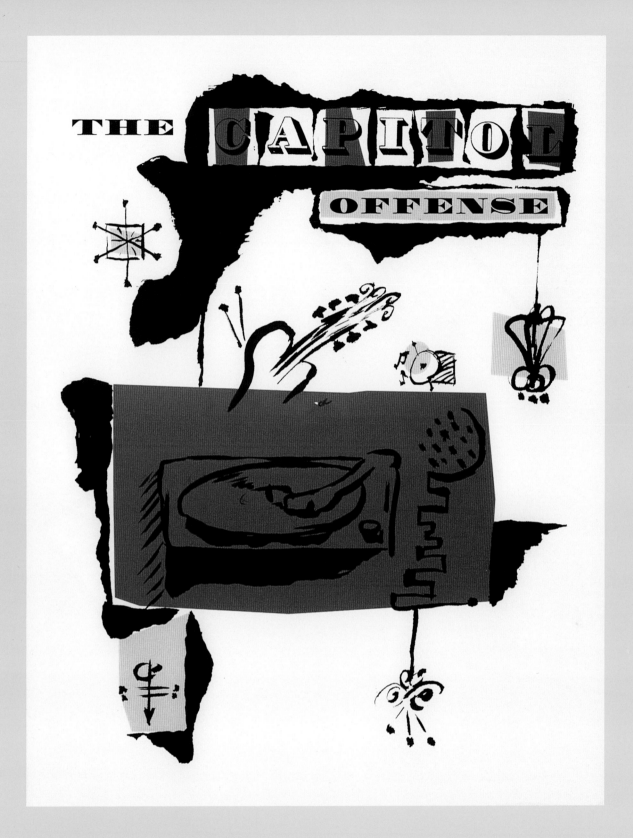

Title: The Capitol Offense Magazine Cover
Design Firm: Modern Dog, Seattle, Washington, USA
Art Director: Jeff Fey, Michael Strassburger
Designer: Michael Strassburger
Client: Capitol Records

The combination of the real with the theoretical is galvanized through a vision that stresses imagination as well as absurdity.

Title: WRGC 45th Anniversary Promotion
Design Firm: Sayles Graphic Design, Des Moines, Iowa, USA
Art Director: John Sayles
Designer: John Sayles
Copywriter: Sheree Clark
Client: Western Regional Greek Conference

The power of type and limited color is expressively conveyed in this striking campaign that links multiple pieces with an unmistakable theme.

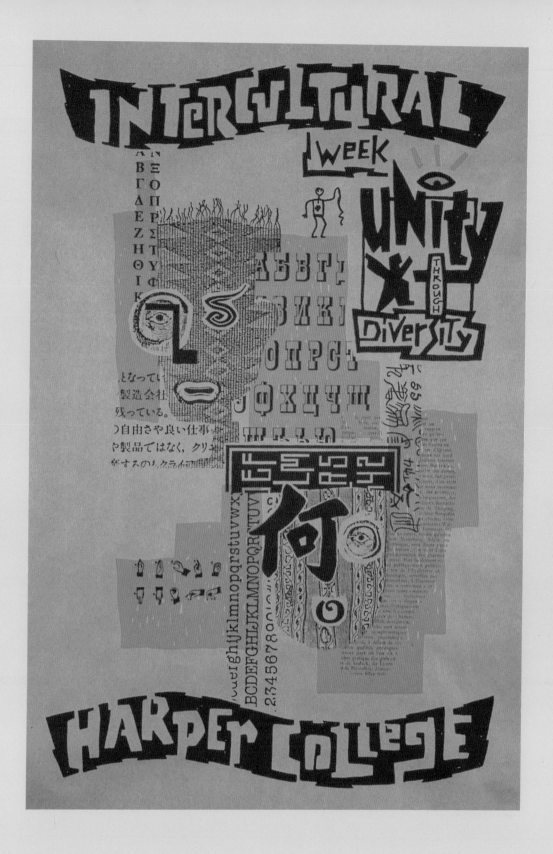

Title: Unity Through Diversity Poster
Design Firm: Sayles Graphic Design, Des Moines, Iowa, USA
Art Director: John Sayles
Designer: John Sayles
Client: Harper College

With only a couple of colors and a global concept, this poster reveals a great deal immediately, but uncovers much more with continued deliberation. Its effective delivery ensures a contempo look that won't age quickly.

**Title: Vaughn/Wedeen Creative Christmas
1993 Promotion**
Design Firm: Vaughn/Wedeen Creative, Albuquerque,
New Mexico, USA
Art Director: Rick Vaughn
Designers: Rick Vaughn, Nicky Ovitt
Hand Lettering: Nicky Ovitt
Client: Vaughn/Wedeen Creative

A holiday greeting in the spirit of the season — staff members
made their favorite dessert and samples were sent to clients in
festive packaging.

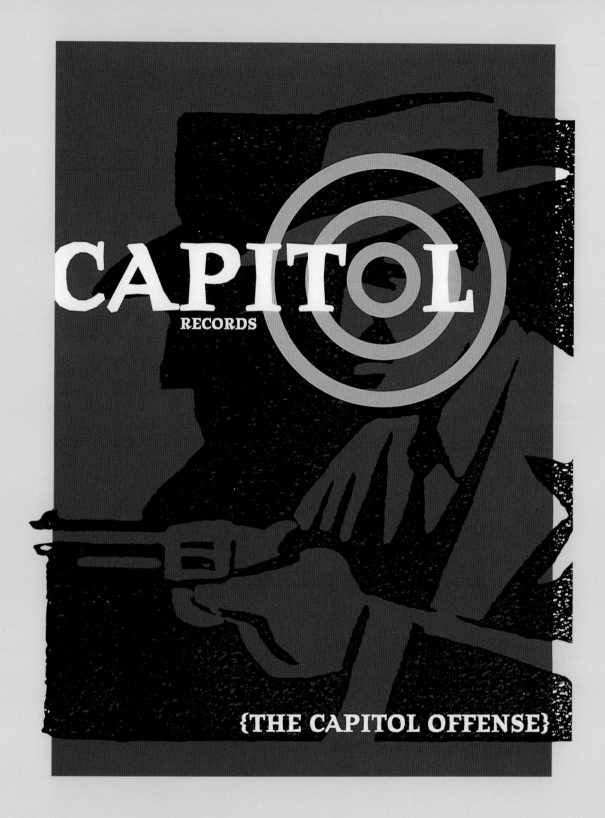

CAPITOL
RECORDS

{THE CAPITOL OFFENSE}

Title: The Capitol Offense 60s Spy Thriller Magazine Cover
Design Firm: Modern Dog, Seattle, Washington, USA
Art Directors: Jeff Fey, Robynne Raye
Designer: Robynne Raye
Client: Capitol Records

The menacing gun, the inauspicious bull's-eye, the ominous silhouette — this design not only demands attention, it sets the aura for collusion and conspiracy, which may be averted, or embraced.

Title: Sandjam '93 Poster
Design Firm: Sayles Graphic Design, Des Moines, Iowa, USA
Art Director: John Sayles
Designer: John Sayles
Client: American Institute of Architects

Sandjam is an annual midwestern event as well as an artistic adventure, and these animated posters and T-shirts convey its gaiety in their flurry of lines and variety of perspective. Two colors give the impelling illusion of many more.

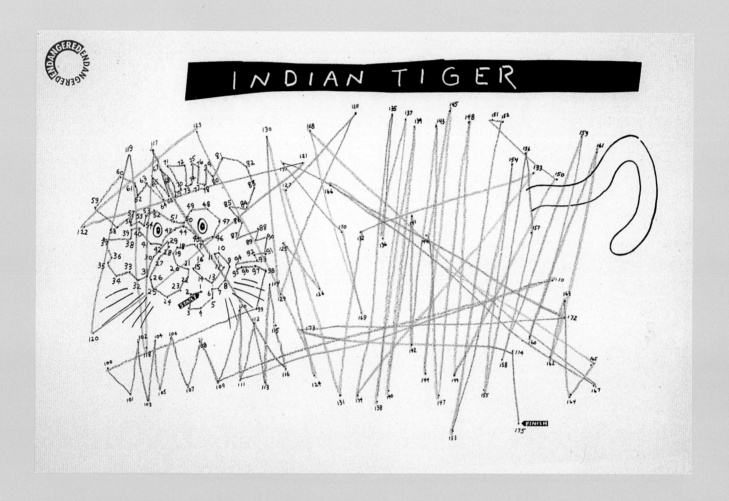

Title: Endangered Indian Tiger Poster
Design Firm: Sommese Design,
State College, Pennsylvania, USA
Art Director: Lanny Sommese
Designer: Lanny Sommese
Client: Pennsylvania State University Institute for Arts and
Humanistic Studies

What can be produced with candor and restraint? A "line drawing" — of sorts — that locates a picture of an endangered species within an innovative concept.

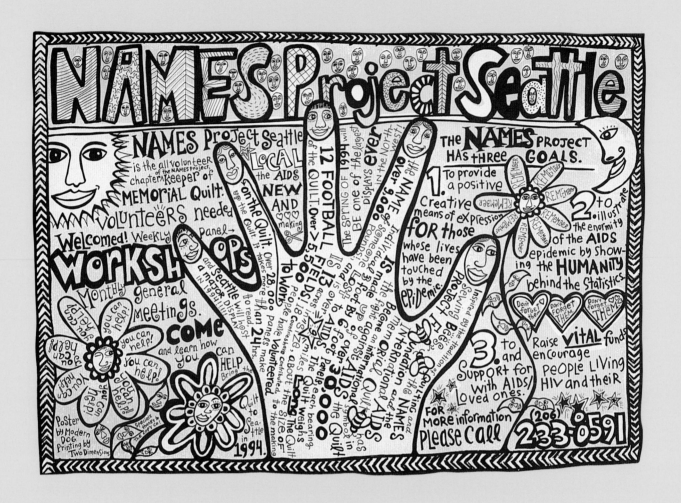

Title: NAMES Project Seattle Information Poster
Design Firm: Modern Dog, Seattle, Washington, USA
Art Director: Robynne Raye, Dan Ripley
Designer: Robynne Raye
Client: NAMES Project Seattle

A lot of information in a pleasing and winsome design, where the sun, moon, and flowers take on a life of their own and entreat the viewer to unhurriedly read and ponder.

Title: "Trademarks" Self-promotion
Design Firm: Dale Vermeer Design, Honolulu, Hawaii, USA
Art Director: Dale Vermeer
Designer: Dale Vermeer
Client: Dale Vermeer Design

A self-promotion that downplays color in favor of producing a well-designed, elegant booklet for very little money. A design that eschews trendiness and spiral binding mean this piece will remain current and new logos can be added whenever desired.

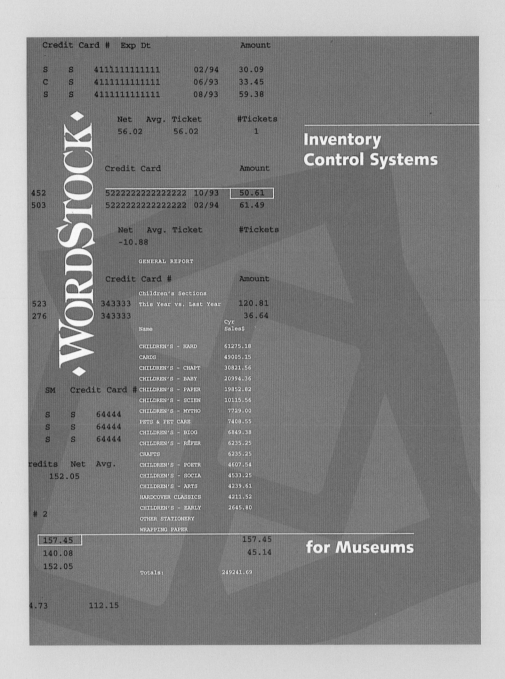

Title: WordStock Product Brochure
Design Firm: Barrett Design, Cambridge, Massachusetts, USA
Art Director: Karen Denely
Designer: Nadine Flowers
Photographer: David Comb
Client: WordStock

Part of the challenge in cover design is to draw in the reader while appearing to enhance the contents inside. Here, green and blue arouse the eye and thoughtfully placed type evoke interest in the figures, rather than apathy.

Title: Aurelia Papitto Artists' Representative Self-Promotion
Design Firm: Eymer Design, Boston, Massachusetts, USA
Art Director: Selene Carro-Eymer
Designer: Selene Carro-Eymer
Client: Aurelia Papitto Artists' Representative

"If it ends well, then it is well," notes the last page of this spirited booklet, and it does more than end well — this charming promotion says all the right things in well-worded quotes and good-natured icons.

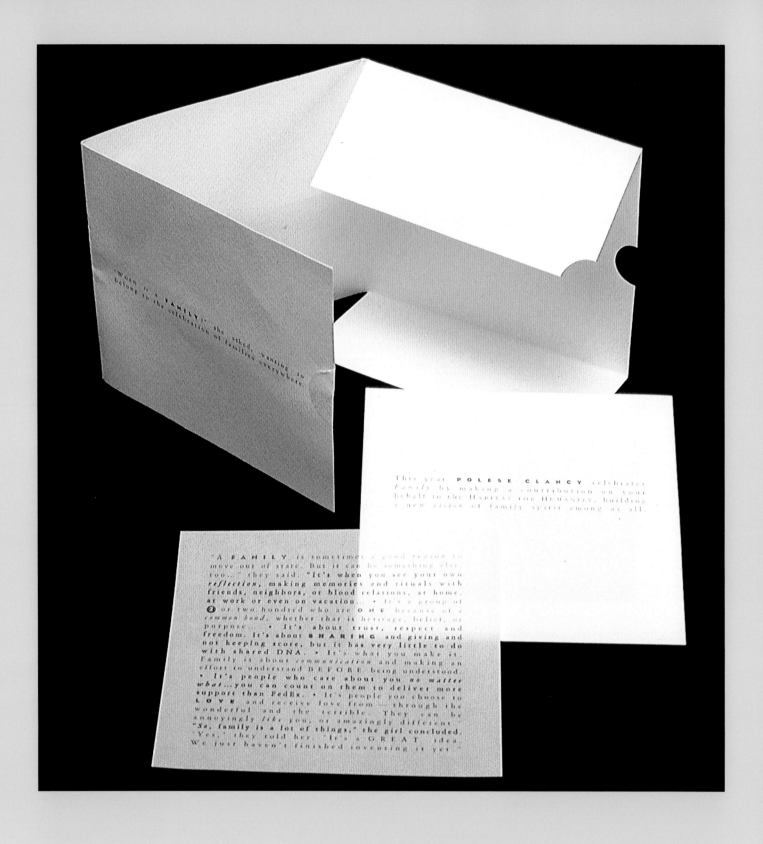

Title: 1993 Holiday Card
Design Firm: Polese Clancy, Inc., Boston, Massachusetts, USA
Art Director: Ellen Clancy
Designer: Ellen Clancy
Client: Polese Clancy, Inc.

A fabulous concept that both touches the heart and embraces the world. Thoughtfully worded text and a translucent inner page combined with a card are unified to offer a message of hope.

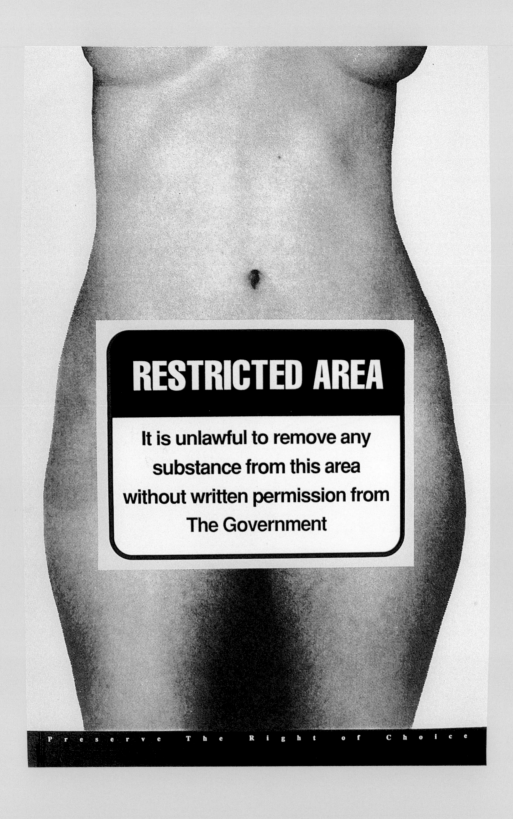

Title: Preserve The Right of Choice Poster
Design Firm: Trudy Cole-Zielanski Design,
Mount Solon, Virginia, USA
Art Director: Trudy Cole-Zielanski
Designer: Trudy Cole-Zielanski
Photographer: Roni Breza
Client: Trudy Cole-Zielanski

When developing this poster addressing a social concern,
two colors were used to help let the sign stand out, and a
monotone was chosen so the photograph did not become
too realistic and stayed "posterish."

Title: Ellery Eskelin "Premonition" CD
Design Firm: Jennifer Juliano, Rutherford, New Jersey, USA
Art Director: Jennifer Juliano
Designer: Jennifer Juliano
Line Art: Stephen Byram
Client: Ellery Eskelin

A provocative representation of the distinctive music of a tenor saxophonist, using an engrossing color combination to add a bit of personality.

ウーマン・イン・ブラック［黒い服の女］ 1992年8月1日［土］―26日［水］ 出演＝萩原流行/斎藤晴彦 PARCO劇場

Title: The Woman in Black Poster Series
Design Firm: Hiromura Design Office, Tokyo, Japan
Art Director: Massaki Hiromura
Designers: Massaki Hiromura, Nubuhiko Aizawa
Client: Parco Co., Ltd.

If dread had a color, it would be black; pain, in this poster, is portrayed as red. Another in a grim, mood-establishing series of posters.

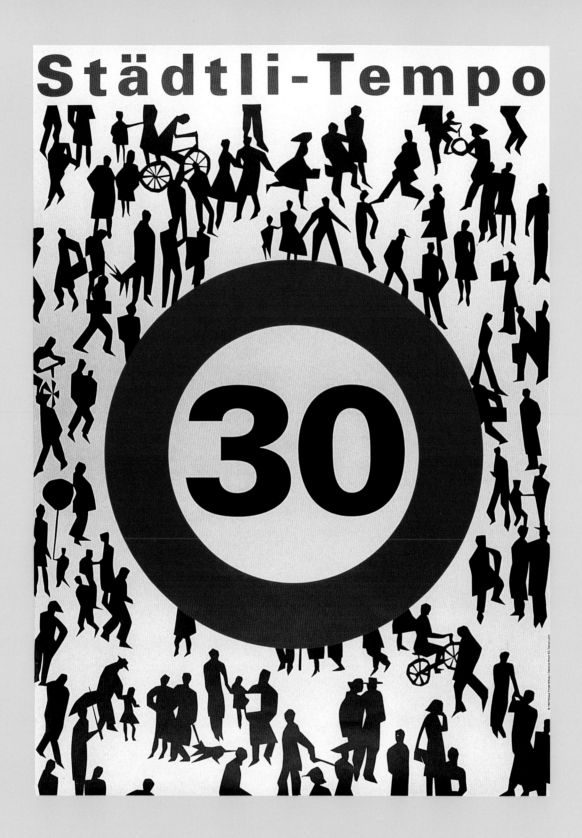

Title: Städtli-Tempo 30 Poster
Design Firm: Niklaus Troxler Design Studio,
Willisau, Switzerland
Art Director: Niklaus Troxler
Designer: Niklaus Troxler
Client: Gemeinde Willisau-Stadt

Here is an example of a visual that the audience can study and continuously discover new details. This poster, ringed by illustrations, also makes a bold statement at its heart.

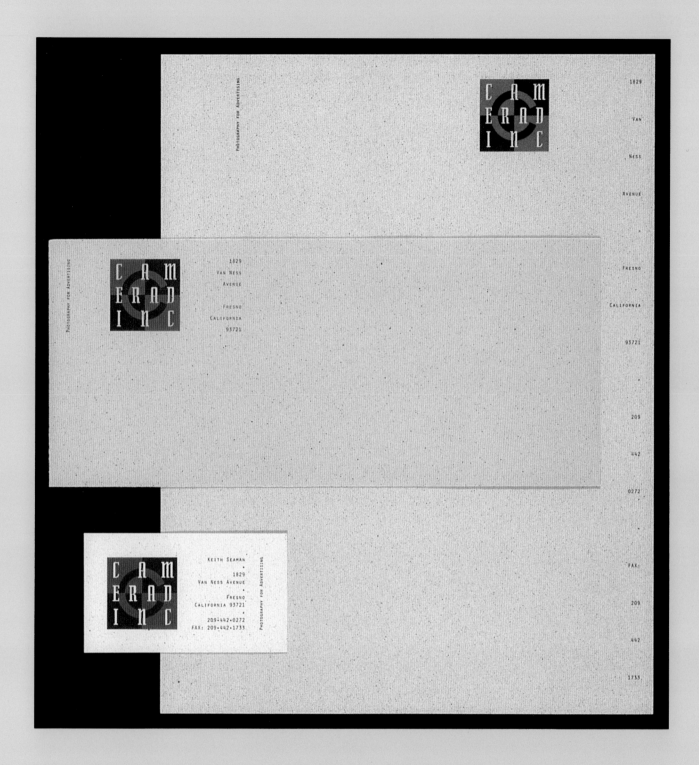

Title: Camerad Logo/Stationery
Design Firm: Shields Design, Fresno, California, USA
Art Director: Charles Shields
Designer: Charles Shields
Client: Camerad Inc.

Paper products that incorporate allusions to the camera lens, excellent design, and a brilliant spectrum of color are all used with vibrant two-color sets on each piece.

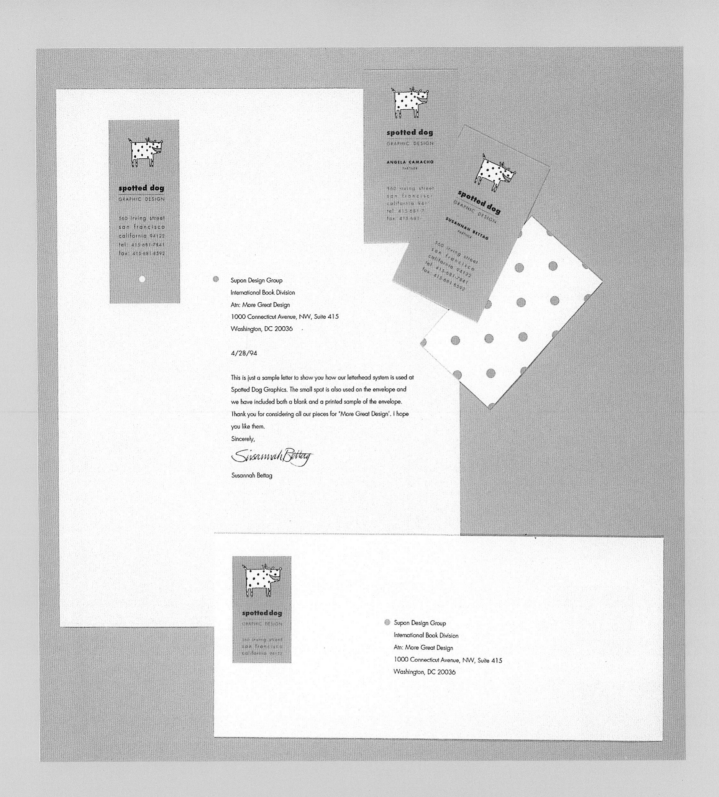

Title: Spotted Dog Letterhead System
Design Firm: Spotted Dog Graphics,
San Francisco, California, USA
Art Directors: Susannah Bettag, Angela Camacho
Designer: Susannah Bettag
Client: Spotted Dog Graphics

The small dot (or "spot") is also used on the envelope in this wonderful visual system that demonstrates the creative range of a design firm.

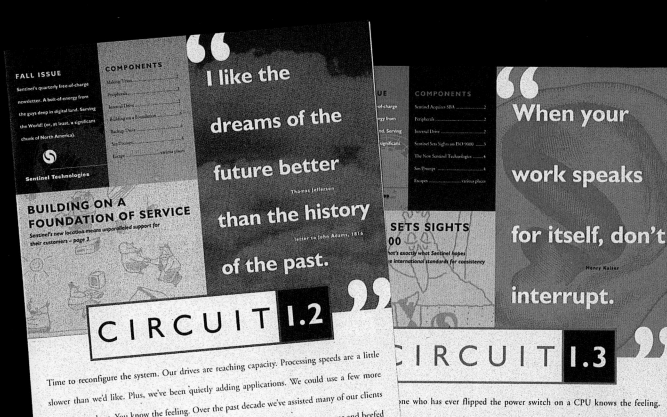

CIRCUIT 1.2

FALL ISSUE

Sentinel's quarterly free-of-charge newsletter. A bolt-of-energy from the guys deep in digital land. Serving the World! (or, at least, a significant chunk of North America).

Sentinel Technologies

COMPONENTS

Making Tracks ....
Peripherals ....
Internal Drive ....
Building on a Foundation ....
Backup Drive ....
See/Prompt ....
Escape ....various places

BUILDING ON A FOUNDATION OF SERVICE

Sentinel's new location means unparalleled support for their customers – page 3

"I like the dreams of the future better than the history of the past."

Thomas Jefferson
letter to John Adams, 1816

Time to reconfigure the system. Our drives are reaching capacity. Processing speeds are a little slower than we'd like. Plus, we've been quietly adding applications. We could use a few more megs, everywhere. You know the feeling. Over the past decade we've assisted many of our clients in upgrading their systems. Now it was our turn. We increased our computing power and beefed up our communication system. But we didn't stop there. We found a bigger building and designed the space so all our people could happily coexist on one well integrated 50,000+ square-foot platform. Then we took a look at our name. "Sentinel Computer Services." We were actually more than that. More proactive. More responsive. So we changed our corporate name to Sentinel *Technologies* and created a new identity system. This issue's Special Edition insert will help explain why. It's still Sentinel, just more of it. We realize we're hitting our customers with a lot of change, but it's change for the better, because we can now give you better service, faster. It's a new configuration we're proud to introduce in this Fall's release of Circuit 1.2.

CIRCUIT 1.3

COMPONENTS

Sentinel Acquires SBA 2
Peripherals 2
Internal Drive 2
Sentinel Sets Sights on ISO 9000 3
The New Sentinel Technologies 4
See/Prompt 4
Escapes ....various places

"When your work speaks for itself, don't interrupt."

Henry Kaiser

SETS SIGHTS
00

...hat's exactly what Sentinel hopes
...he international standards for consistency

... one who has ever flipped the power switch on a CPU knows the feeling. ...mory checks, system checks, and all the other start-up diagnostics to cycle ...e sensation when we first activated Sentinel Technologies. The new name. ...n telecommunications system. Improved meeting facilities. Fully equipped ...xpanded parts department. A hardware/software demonstration area. An ...vice center. We're powered up and the configuration is working well. But ...t just a few months ago this was all specs on a blueprint. Now it feels as ...air of blue jeans. It's even more amazing to think back 11 years — when ...ts on a small office with six people. And even though the company has ...) employees and three service divisions, we are working together more ...... all our customers. In short, we're pleased to report that all systems are go, access times are faster than ever, and we're not only networking, we're teamworking.

Title: Circuit Newsletter
Design Firm: Pagliuco Design Company, Chicago, Illinois, USA
Art Director: Michael Pagliuco
Designer: Michael Pagliuco
Illustrators: Steve Gill, Paul Moch
Copywriter: Charles Couri
Client: Sentinel Technologies

This newsletter for a computer sales and service firm updates itself quarterly (version 1.2, 1.3, etc.), uses "Components" for "Departments," and an "Enter" keypad illustration to let readers know when to turn the page. Colors were linked to the seasons.

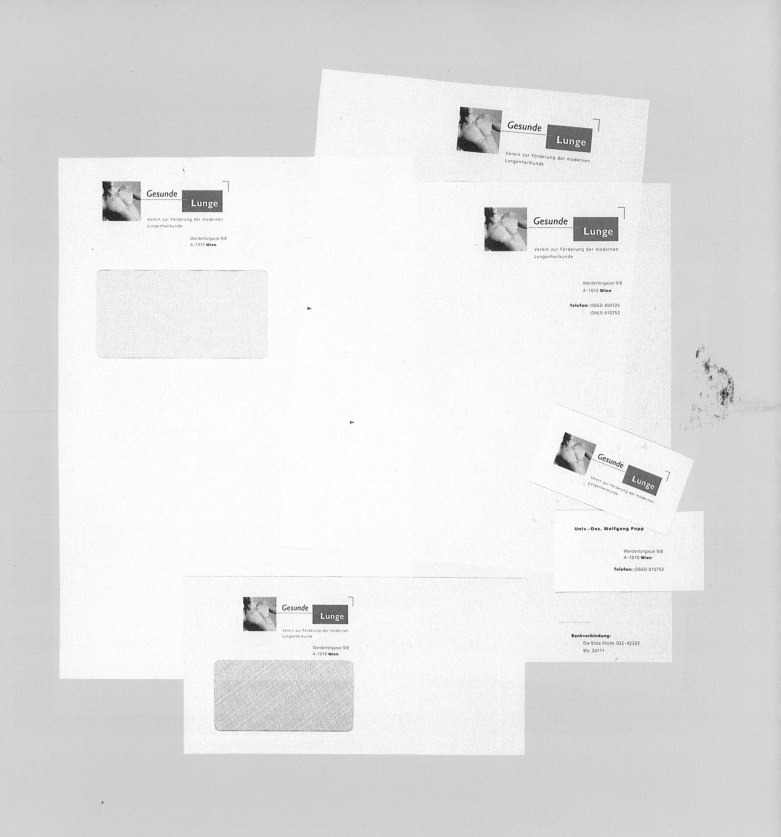

Title: Gesunde Lunge (Healthy Lungs) Stationery
Design Firm: Atelier Heider, Vienna, Austria
Art Director: Clemens Heider
Designer: Clemens Heider
Photographer: Harald Bauer
Client: Welldone Vienna

A contemporary but spare approach that communicates both the requisite information about and the positive intent of an organization.

Title: Invitation to a Dialogue Brochure
Design Firm: Atelier Heider, Vienna, Austria
Art Director: Clemens Heider
Designer: Clemens Heider
Client: Prima Public Relations

This elaborate cover works with a brochure that is unusually trimmed so that the navy blue square, its type, and the tissue band become the dominant elements in a powerful design.

Title: Bedford Falls Logo and Stationery
Design Firm: Jay Vigon Design Studio,
Studio City, California, USA
Art Director: Jay Vigon
Designer: Jay Vigon
Client: Bedford Falls Film Company

A shrewd visual (look closely to find the second initial) is an important component of the stylish paper products that include a double-sided business card.

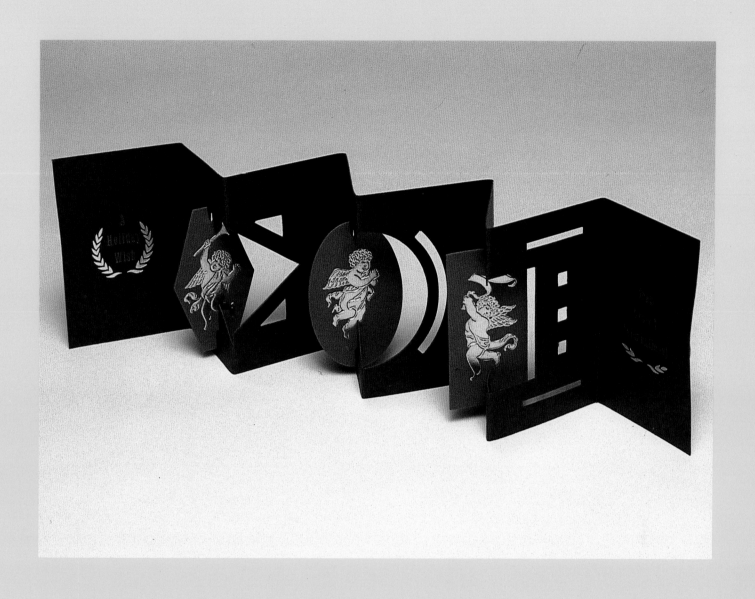

Title: 1993 Christmas Card
Design Firm: Julia Tam Design, Palos Verdes, California, USA
Art Director: Julia Chong Tam
Designer: Julia Chong Tam
Client: Team 7 International

Festive colors and moving, gilded angels customize this holiday greeting that features joyful good wishes in a splendid package.

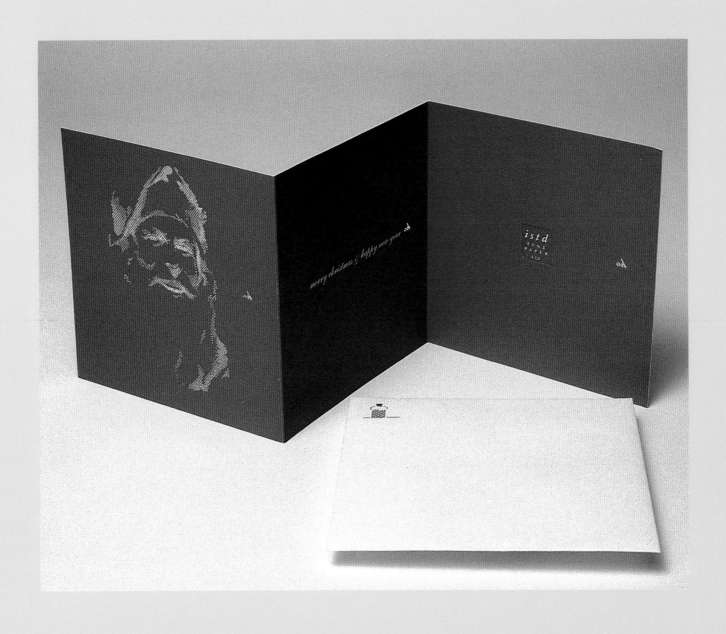

Title: ISTD Christmas Card
Design Firm: Trickett & Webb, London, England
Designers: Lynn Trickett, Brian Webb, Martin Cox
Client: ISTD Fine Paper

A tiny, laser-cut red chimney adorns the envelope and a message inside ensures the smiling Santa won't remain silent in this remarkable piece, which uses a few simple elements for a very special result.

Title: Institute of Pediatrics Medical University of Lodz Stationery
Design Firm: Atelier Tadeusz Piechura, Lodz, Poland
Art Director: Tadeusz Piechura
Designer: Tadeusz Piechura
Client: Instytut Pediatrii Akademii Medycznej w Lodzi

Bright white backgrounds, carefully placed rules, corresponding type, and a logo that projects the feel of promise and confidence characterize these papers.

Title: After Hours Stationery
Design Firm: After Hours, Phoenix, Arizona, USA
Art Directors: Russ Haan, Dino Paul
Designers: Dino Paul, Brad Smith, Todd Fedell
Photographer: Kevin Cruff
Client: After Hours

Using one side for phone and fax numbers and the other for address, this stationery sheet becomes a balanced piece, playing with the "time" theme but achieving its true sagacity in its careful use of restraint.

Title: Vida Restaurant Logo and Stationery Design
Design Firm: Jay Vigon Studio, Studio City, California, USA
Art Director: Fred Eric
Designer: Jay Vigon
Client: Vida Restaurant

The burnished orbs provide an ideal California complement to papers that communicate a bit of extravagance as well as tasteful understatement.

Title: Unfettered Photographs Promotion Campaign
Design Firm: The Q Design Group Ltd.,
Wilton, Connecticut, USA
Art Director: Susan Caldwell
Designer: Susan Caldwell
Photographer: Michael Heintz
Copywriters: Charyn Atkin, Howard V. Sann
Client: New Canaan Society for the Arts

The campaign is a gently tinged collection of cards, posters,
and an ingenious booklet, all sharing lyrical photos and a
chorus of well-written information, theories, and dreams.

Title: The Ballsun Company Corporate ID
Design Firm: Spotted Dog Graphics,
San Francisco, California, USA
Art Directors: Susannah Bettag, Angela Camacho
Designer: Susannah Bettag
Client: The Ballsun Company

From letterhead to mailing label, this modern conceit is a
thoroughly tasteful work whose dynamic border sets off a
wonderful design.

Signature & Color Scheme

Incorrected Symbol

MONKEY'92

Monkey Red

Monkey Gray

MONKEY'92

MONKEY'92

MONKEY'92

Title: Christmas Card ('91)
Design Firm: Dookim Design, Seoul, Korea
Art Director: Doo H. Kim
Designers: Dongil Lee, Sung Hee Lee, Jiwon Shin
Client: Dookim Design

A tongue-in-cheek guidebook of corporate design is strengthened by exceptional choice of color and attention to detail, such as the silver envelope sticker.

Title: Mujirushiryohin Sales Promotion Items
Design Firm: Hiromura Design Office, Tokyo, Japan
Art Director: Massaki Hiromura
Creative Directors: Ikko Tanaka, Kazuko Koike
Designers: Massaki Hiromura, Toshiyuki Kojima
Illustrator: Michael Bartaros
Client: The Ryohinkeikaku, Ltd.

Comical illustrations work with clever captions in this series
of matching but very diverse promotional pieces, each produced
with a unique two-color combination.

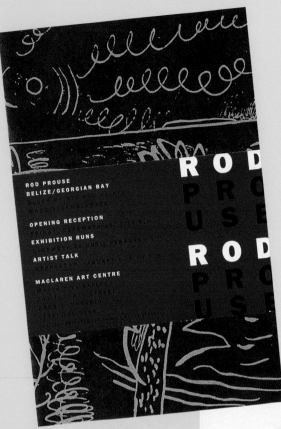

'Bay with Barracuda'
1993 Block Print 45" x 60"

Title: Rod Prouse Catalog
Design Firm: Constructive Communications,
Mississauga, Ontario, Canada
Designer: Tracey Watt
Printer: LithoSource
Client: MacLaren Art Centre

An exhibit of block prints and painted wood artworks is
enhanced by an accompanying piece whose subdued colors
are set off by a bold band of red that delivers the details
in a visionary way.

114

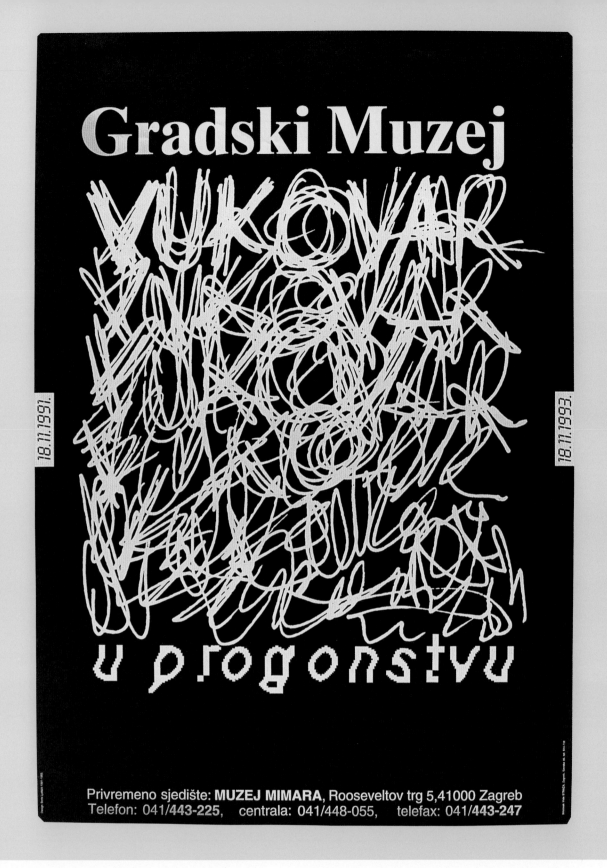

Title: Municipal Museum of Vukovar in Exile Poster
Design Firm: Studio International, Zagreb, Croatia
Art Director: Boris Ljubicic
Client: The Municipal Museum of Vukovar

The Croatian town of Vukovar was destroyed by war in 1991 and its museum was razed to the ground. The new town logo is a graphic representation of the disappearance of Vukovar, its culture, and museum. The black background with the logo in negative (i.e., white) and embossed in gold represents Vukovar's tragedy.

ウーマン・イン・ブラック［黒い服の女］1992年8月1日［土］—26日［水］ 出演＝萩原流行／斎藤晴彦 PARCO劇場

Title: The Woman in Black Poster Series
Design Firm: Hiromura Design Office, Tokyo, Japan
Art Director: Massaki Hiromura
Designers: Massaki Hiromura, Nubuhiko Aizawa
Client: Parco Co., Ltd.

A savage and ominous tone unfolds from this poster's artful contrast with dark on light and the slash of red rising like an apparition from its center.

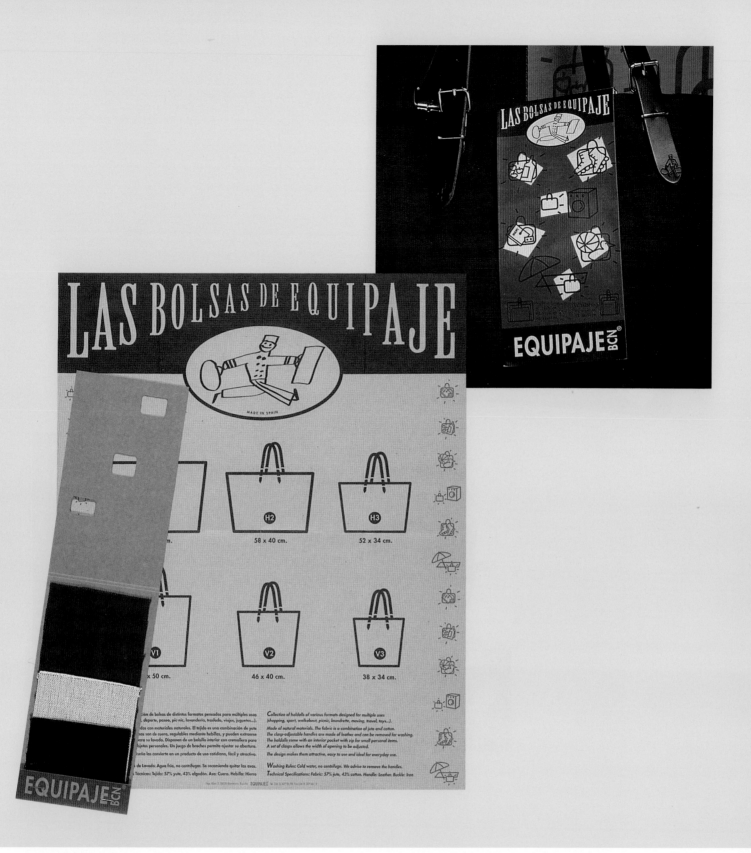

Title: Las Bolsas de Equipaje Promotion
Design Firm: Sonsoles Llorens, Barcelona, Spain
Art Director: Sonsoles Llorens
Designer: Sonsoles Llorens
Client: Félix Preciado Equipaje BCN

A collection of bags made of natural materials is promoted with a well-suited campaign that displays the products from different perspectives, giving them a dashing, cosmopolitan appeal.

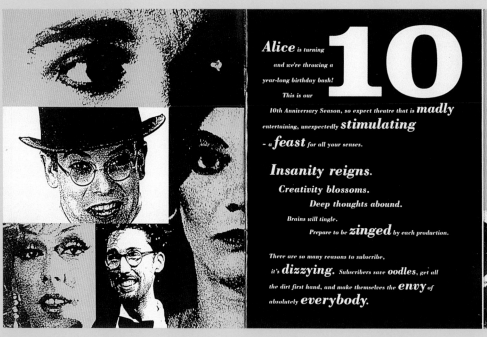

Alice *is turning* and *we're throwing a year-long birthday bash!* This is our **10**

10th Anniversary Season, so expect theatre that is **madly** *entertaining, unexpectedly* **stimulating** - *a* ***feast*** *for all your senses.*

Insanity reigns.

Creativity blossoms.

Deep thoughts abound.

Brains will tingle.

Prepare to be ***zinged*** *by each production.*

There are so many reasons to subscribe, it's **dizzying.** *Subscribers save* **oodles**, *get all the dirt first hand, and make themselves the* **envy** *of absolutely* **everybody.**

Title: Alice B. Theatre Season Brochure
Design Firm: Modern Dog, Seattle, Washington, USA
Art Director: Vittorio Costarella
Designer: Vittorio Costarella
Client: Alice B. Theatre

Here is a piece as enterprising as the organization it promotes. On the occasion of a theatre's 10th birthday, upcoming shows are accompanied by adventurous images.

Title: Wedding Invitation
Design Firm: Lambert Design Studio, Dallas, Texas, USA
Art Director: Joy Cathey
Designer: Joy Cathey
Client: Joy Cathey and Scott Price

A genteel design commemorates a wedding with associated pieces and a gift for the guests — petunia seeds housed in a trim packet adorned with ribbon.

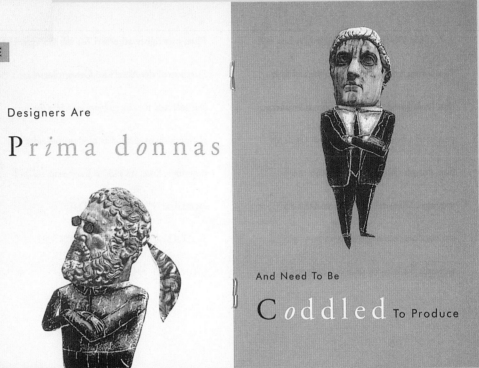

Title: Annual Report Myths Promotion
Design Firm: Corporate Reports, Atlanta, Georgia, USA
Art Director: Brant Day
Copywriter: Sandy Dempsey
Client: Corporate Reports

This self-promotion for a studio specializing in annual reports takes a humorous perspective, using amusing figures to market a timely, good-natured message.

Title: Kara Gala Invitation
Design Firm: Karin Scholz Design, Palo Alto, California, USA
Art Director: Karin Scholz
Designer: Karin Scholz
Client: Kara

A dramatic, golden invitation that unfolds to proclaim a benefit event. A dazzling piece with a look of royalty that almost glimmers.

Title: Pacific Coast Financial Securities Letterhead
Design Firm: White Design, Long Beach, California, USA
Art Director: John White
Designer: Aram Youssefian
Client: Pacific Coast Financial Securities

A truly classic statement, letterhead is organized inside an eloquent folder of soft shades that creates an impression of lavishness.

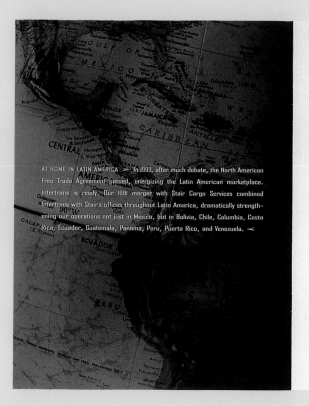

Title: **Intertrans 1993 Annual Report**
Design Firm: SullivanPerkins, Dallas, Texas, USA
Art Directors: Ron Sullivan, Dan Richards
Designer: Dan Richards
Photographer: Gerry Kano
Copywriters: Hilary Kennard, Mark Perkins
Client: Intertrans

The green of currency and the black of finesse and ultimate professionalism combine in this original approach to an annual report.

Title: Sackett Design Associates Business Papers
Design Firm: Sackett Design Associates,
San Francisco, California, USA
Art Director: Mark Sackett
Designer: Mark Sackett
Client: Sackett Design Associates

Just when print products start to look similar, along comes
this polished, svelte image, created from deep, civilized colors,
culminating in its uncharacteristically slender business card.

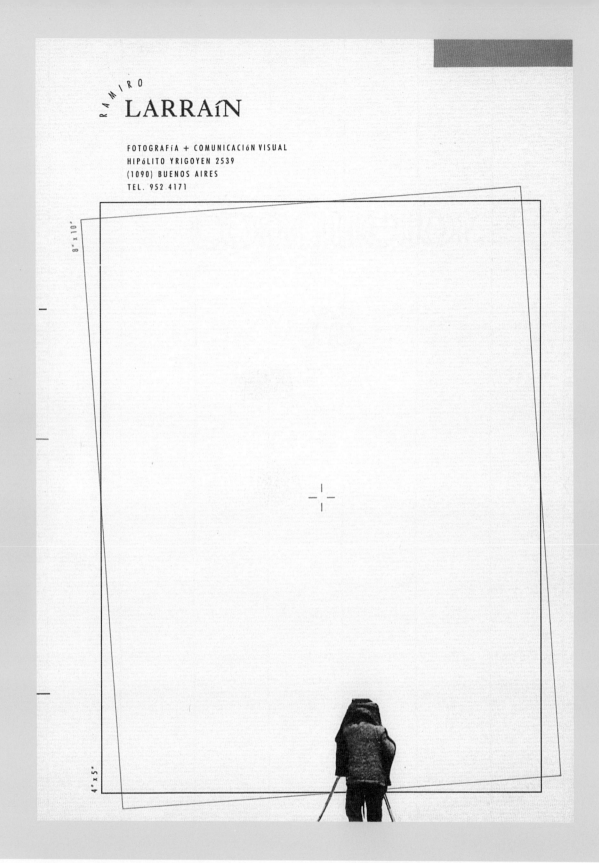

RAMIRO
LARRAíN

FOTOGRAFíA + COMUNICACIóN VISUAL
HIPóLITO YRIGOYEN 2539
(1090) BUENOS AIRES
TEL. 952.4171

Title: **Ramiro Larraín Letterhead**
Design Firm: Daniel Higa, Buenos Aires, Argentina
Art Director: Daniel Higa
Designer: Daniel Higa
Client: Ramiro Larraín

This design introduces a practical page that makes clever use of a photograph and careful arrangement of color to ensure the photography theme is apparent but not excessive.

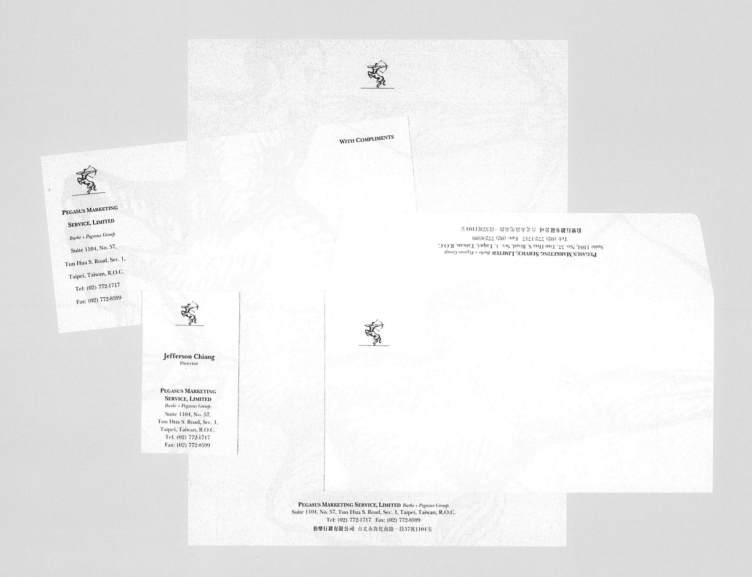

Title: Pegasus Marketing Service Limited Stationery
Design Firm: Leslie Chan Design Co. Ltd.,
Taipei, Taiwan, Republic of China
Art Director: Chan Wing Kei. Leslie
Designers: Chan Wing Kei. Leslie, Tong Song Wei
Client: Pegasus Marketing Service Limited

A well-crafted design that demonstrates gracious imaging using delicate tones and hues, and discriminating logo placement.

415 East
Olive Avenue

Fresno
California
93728

209-497-8060

FAX
209-497-8061

Charles Shields

415 East Olive Avenue
Fresno, California 93728
209-497-8060
FAX: 209-497-8061

Title: Shields Design Stationery
Design Firm: Shields Design, Fresno, California, USA
Art Director: Charles Shields
Designer: Charles Shields
Client: Shields Design

With a handsome choice of paper and complementary colors on the business card, letterhead, and envelope, these business papers are not only appropriate, but novel and progressive as well.

127

Title: A Masked Ball Invitation
Design Firm: Wright Communications,
New York, New York, USA
Art Director: Nanette Wright
Designer: Janice Comes
Client: The Holy Trinity Neighborhood Center

The riddle of the masked ball becomes reality using deep,
sleight-of-hand colors and type that magically appears
on a dark page.

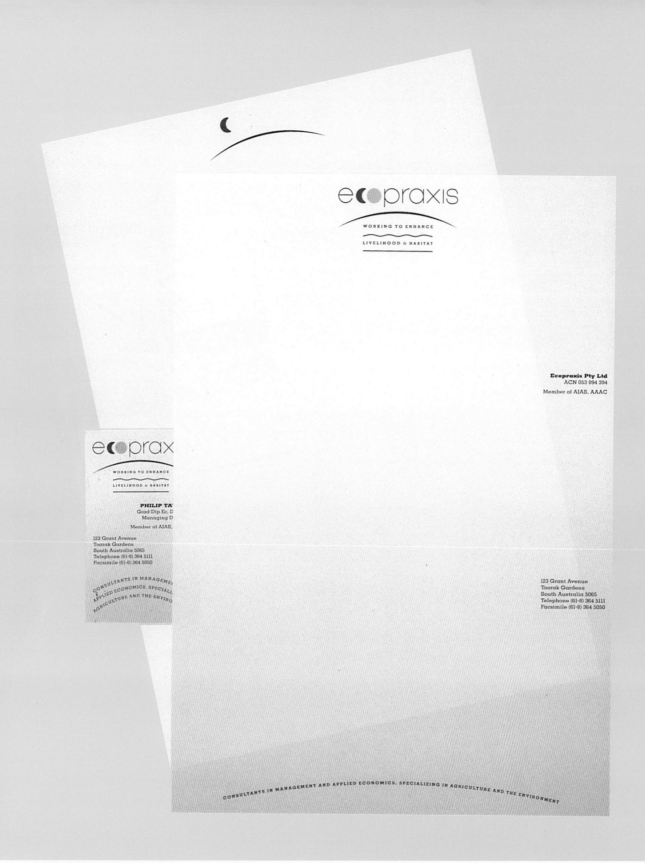

Title: Ecopraxis Stationery
Design Firm: Burton Nesbitt Graphic Design,
Adelaide, South Australia, Australia
Art Director: Burton Nesbitt Graphic Design
Designer: Burton Nesbitt Graphic Design
Printer: Five Star Press
Client: Ecopraxis Pty Ltd

Pale, modified earth tones and an inspired use of logo elements create a fine solution for a consultancy concentrating on the environment and agriculture.

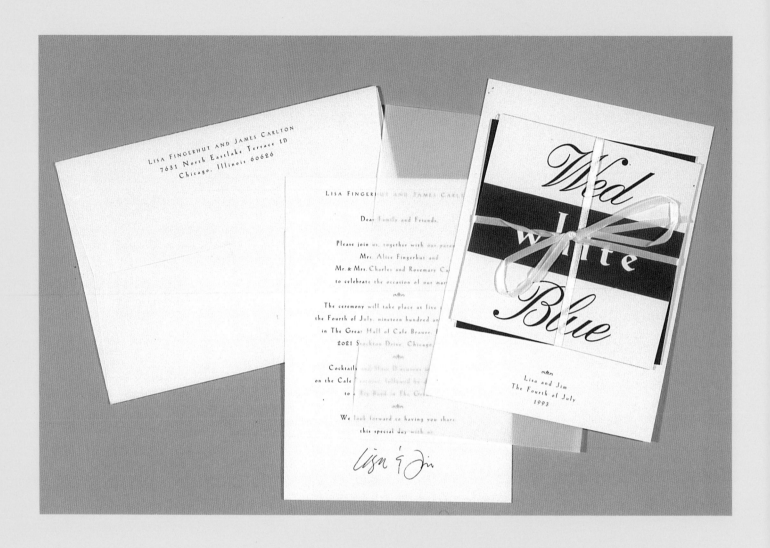

Title: **Wedding Invitation**
Design Firm: Design Horizons International,
Chicago, Illinois, USA
Art Director: Jim Carlton
Designer: Jim Carlton
Client: Jim Carlton and Lisa Fingerhut

A collection of red, white, and blue information and response cards tied with ribbon make becoming elements and adhere to the patriotic theme — a natural choice for a Fourth of July wedding.

Title: Historic Hawaii Invitation
Design Firm: Dale Vermeer Design, Honolulu, Hawaii, USA
Art Director: Dale Vermeer
Designer: Dale Vermeer
Illustrator: Delro Rosco
Client: Historic Hawaii Foundation

Each panel of this fold-out brochure was carefully conceived to arrive at an extraordinary piece, whose bold graphics and cover illustration summarize the spirit of the event.

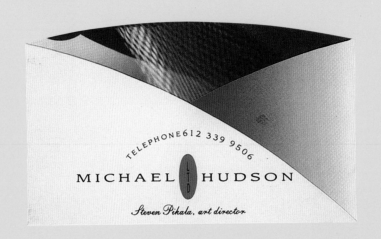

Title: Michael Hudson, Ltd. Business Card
Design Firm: Michael Hudson, Ltd.,
Minneapolis, Minnesota, USA
Art Director: Michael Hudson
Designer: Michael Hudson
Client: Michael Hudson, Ltd.

We haven't found a person yet who isn't immediately impressed with the originality of this unorthodox business card, combining a photo with graphics and dimension.

MERIT
1·2 & 3
COLORS

Blue
288

Violet
2543

Orange
1655

Washington by Night

Vintage Photographs from the 30s *by* VOLKMAR WENTZEL ❧ Introduction *by* JAMES GOODE

Title: Washington By Night Book
Design Firm: Sicklesmith Design, Washington, D.C., USA
Designer: Donna Sicklesmith
Photographer: Volkmar Wentzel
Client: Starwood Publishing

A treasure trove of tri-tones capturing magnificent capital-city scenes from the 1930s is introduced by a dramatic still and followed by lay-outs that are truly regal.

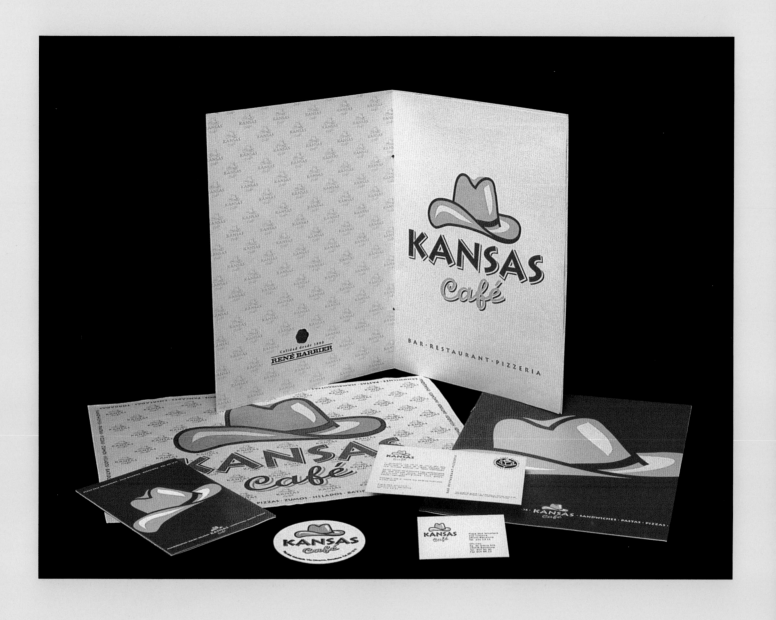

Title: Kansas Café Campaign
Design Firm: Sonsoles Llorens, Barcelona, Spain
Art Director: Sonsoles Llorens
Designer: Sonsoles Llorens
Client: CGN Invest

From placemat to coaster to menu, this print project creates a dynamic effect using three deep colors, repititions of the logo, and a typeface that says "food and fun."

Title: Physician and Patient
Design Firm: Richard Danne & Associates Inc,
New York, New York, USA
Art Director: Richard Danne
Designer: Richard Danne
Photographer: Bill Ballenberg
Client: American Academy on Physician and Patient

It is no easy task to communicate compassion and professionalism in pictures and print. This brochure does so by the use of economy in elements such as color, and by careful arrangement of white space.

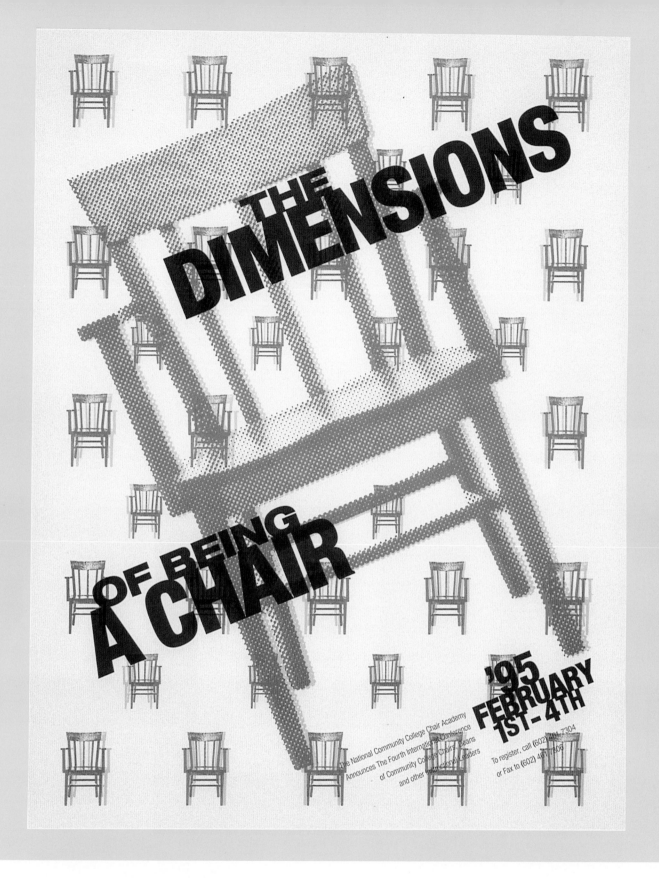

Title: Chair Academy 3-D Poster
Design Firm: After Hours, Phoenix, Arizona, USA
Art Director: Russ Haan
Designers: Dino Paul, Brad Smith, Todd Fedell
Client: National Community College Chair Academy

On this poster, the parameters of the chair are blurred by both line and color, creating an electrifying perspective and drawing the gaze of most passers-by.

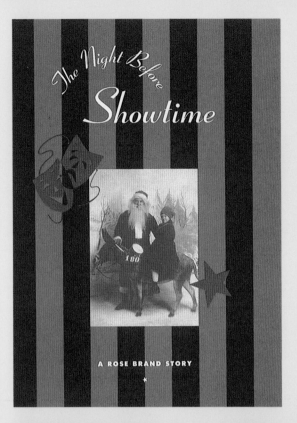

Title: The Night Before Showtime Holiday Greeting
Design Firm: Schowalter2 Design,
Short Hills, New Jersey, USA
Art Director: Toni Schowalter
Designers: Toni Schowalter, Ilene Price
Client: RoseBrand

A Christmas greeting in verse for a purveyor of studio, stage, and scenic supplies, each page displays illustrations of client services in bright colors.

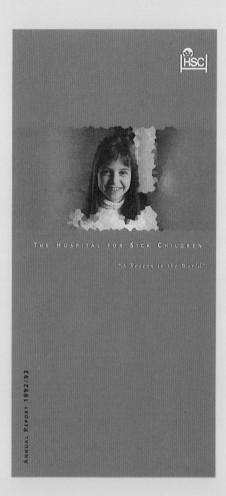

THE HOSPITAL FOR SICK CHILDREN

"A Beacon to the World"

ANNUAL REPORT 1992/93

Approximately ten percent of all children who successfully fight cancer are struck with the disease again within 20 years; an international research team based at Harvard University, but led by HSC physician David Malkin, learned that in some children the second cancer is directly related to a defective gene.

"A drug that should save the government millions of dollars" – that's how Haematologist Nancy Olivieri described the success of the drug L-1 to treat patients with thalassemia major. Seventeen HSC patients are involved in studies with L-1; although it doesn't eradicate thalassemia, it prevents the toxic side effects of treatment.

The New England Journal of Medicine reported on the collaborative research of Dr. Susan Perrine from the Children's Hospital in Oakland and Dr. Nancy Olivieri into the use of butyrate to increase haemoglobin F in patients with thalassemia and sickle cell disease. Results of the drug on one HSC patient were described as "dramatic."

There were other significant research advancements: genetic studies in the chromosomal neighbourhood of the Huntington's disease gene (Dr. Johanna Rommens); how infectious bacteria attach to bacterial cells (Dr. Clifford Lingwood); establishment of transgenic mouse experimental technology (Dr. John Chamberlain); new molecular techniques in medical diagnosis (Drs. Jeremy Squire and Linda Penn); and single-cell ion transport research (Dr. Kevin Foskett).

Special Recognition

Dozens of HSC staff and students received honours, awards, praise and accolades from their peers, professional societies and health care organizations throughout the world. Below, just a few.

Louise Crawford, a teacher of deaf children associated with the Department of Otolaryngology since 1962, was appointed a Member of the Order of Canada for Distinguished Service.

Dr. Manuel Buchwald received the 1992 Fanconi Anemia Award of Merit.

RESEARCH FUNDING
(EXTERNAL GRANTS)

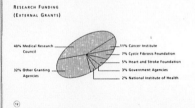

40% Medical Research Council

32% Other Granting Agencies

11% Cancer Institute
7% Cystic Fibrosis Foundation
5% Heart and Stroke Foundation
3% Government Agencies
2% National Institute of Health

Dr. William G. Cole, head of Orthopaedic Surgery, with Jian Lu, research technician

Once Dr. Cole began to discuss a move from his home in Melbourne, Australia, calls of interest came from leading research and health care facilities throughout the world. "Everyone wanted Bill," Dr. James Friesen, director of the Hospital's Research Institute, recalls, "because of his unique talents and skills – orthopaedic surgeon, geneticist, researcher. We are extremely fortunate that he chose to come here, and already we are seeing the benefits for Ontario children, as well as for the world scientific community."

Title: The Hospital for Sick Children Annual Report 1992/93
Design Firm: Eskind Waddell, Toronto, Ontario, Canada
Designer: Donna Gedeon
Client: The Hospital for Sick Children

Use of unexpected borders and type placement create the unusual effects and friendly feel of this practicable annual report.

Will she appear in the Grand Opera as a *prima donna*?

Title: Rachel Brown Birth Announcement
Design Firm: SullivanPerkins, Dallas, Texas, USA
Art Director: Ron Sullivan
Designer: Dan Richards
Copywriters: Dan Richards, Mark Perkins
Client: Bob Davis

The more serious side to this announcement is that, along with high expectations and dreams, parents also experience a few fears and worries about the potential path of their new baby. Pink was an obvious choice for this "pro-bono" project produced for the baby's grandfather.

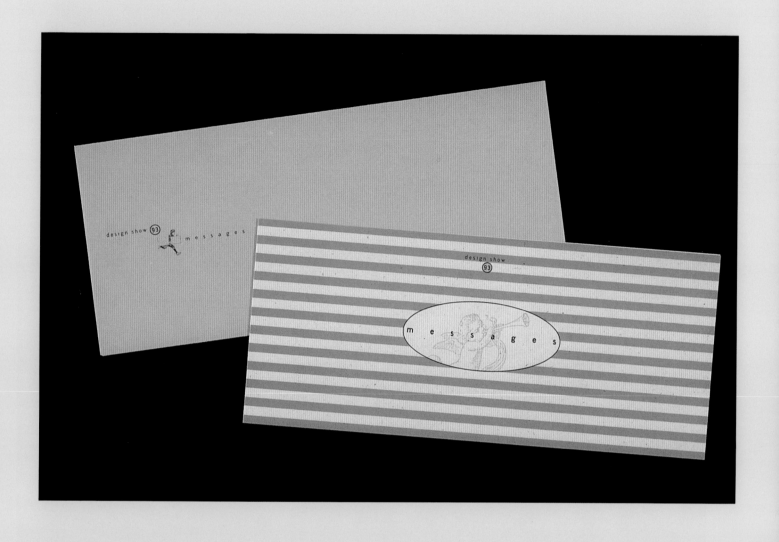

Title: Design Show '93 Inivitation
Design Firm: Mireille Smits Design,
Indianapolis, Indiana, USA
Designer: Mireille Smits

The strategy for this piece was the use of colors untried before in combination, that were also tied to the season of the event. Clip art was gathered from around the world. Type and other elements, like dotted lines, were added to give it a classic, old feel.

Title: Sunrise Greeting Card Box
Design Firm: Mires Design, San Diego, California, USA
Art Director: Scott Mires
Designer: Scott Mires
Illustrator: Tracy Sabin
Client: Sunrise Publications

A box with a touch of the unpretentious, natural, and provincial, it appeals to buyers by creating interest in itself and mystery about the cards it houses.

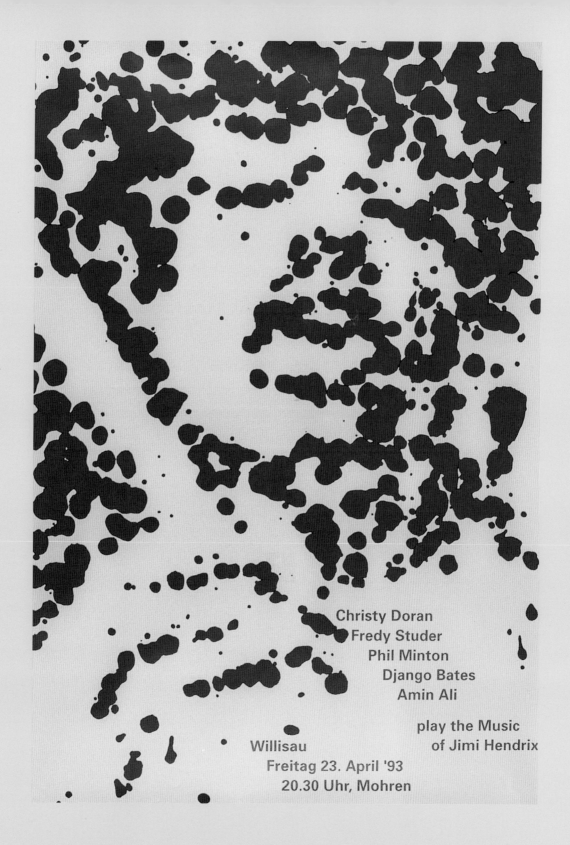

Christy Doran
Fredy Studer
Phil Minton
Django Bates
Amin Ali

play the Music
Willisau   of Jimi Hendrix
Freitag 23. April '93
20.30 Uhr, Mohren

Title: ...Play the Music of Jimi Hendrix Poster
Design Firm: Niklaus Troxler Design Studio,
Willisau, Switzerland
Art Director: Niklaus Troxler
Designer: Niklaus Troxler
Client: Jazz in Willisau

Look carefully, and the image of master guitarist Jimi Hendrix
emerges from a pattern of yellow and blue. The colors convey
the power of the music; the poster heralds a festival where
Hendrix's music can be appreciated worldwide.

Title: MHS 1992 Annual Report
Design Firm: Michael Hudson, Ltd.,
Minneapolis, Minnesota, USA
Art Director: Michael Hudson
Designers: Michael Hudson, Steve Pikala
Client: Minnesota Historical Society

A tissue band imprinted with clouds that depict an unlimited horizon surrounds a print piece that makes excellent restrained use of gold and delivers information and figures with finesse and sophistication.

Title: Holiday Promotion
Design Firm: Design Horizons International,
Chicago, Illinois, USA
Art Director: Krista Ferdinand
Designer: Krista Ferdinand
Client: Design Horizons International

From "Tangy Red Gazpacho" to "Brownie Mint Bar," this booklet makes creative work of the traditional "red and green" holiday theme, topped with a cinnamon stick tied with a red plastic ribbon.

TEATRE INFANTIL A CAN DEU

Diumenge, 28 de març

ES HISTÒRIES DE TAXI MAX

CIA. MARCEL GROS

Diumenge, 25 d'abril

ESTERNUTS

L'ÀVIA PEPA

Diumenge, 30 de maig

RES I SENYORS, AIXÒ ÉS MÀGIA

LA CAPSA MÀGICA

Diumenge, 26 de setembre

ES BREUS I EXTRAORDINARIS

CESC SERRAT

Diumenge, 31 d'octubre

AUBUSTER

ELS ROCAMORA

Diumenge, 28 de novembre

SI PLOU MARXEM

PEP & BOCOI

representacions començaran a les 12 hores.
: Can Deu, Pl. Concòrdia 13. Tel. 410 10 07.

ENTRADA LLIURE

Ajuntament de Barcelona
Districte de les Corts

TEATRE INFANTIL A CAN DEU

Diumenge, 17 d'abril

QUE N'ETS, DE BÈSTIA!

CIA. TEIA MONER

Diumenge, 15 de Maig

PATATIM DE PATATAM A L'ÍNDIA

FLIC-FLAC TEATRE

Diumenge, 19 de juny

SIMFONIA EN FA DE ROBA

MARDUIX

Diumenge, 18 de setembre

EL CIRC MÉS PETITÓ

GERMANS TOTÓ

Diumenge, 16 d'octubre

"A-2"

COMPANYIA ÍNFIMA LA PUÇA

Diumenge, 20 de novembre

LA BALENA ELENA

TITELLES BABI

Diumenge, 18 de desembre

CONTES AL PORTAL

TEATRE DE CORDÓ

Totes les representacions començaran a les 12 hores.
Centre Cívic Can Deu, Pl. Concòrdia 13. Tel. 410 10 07.

PREU ENTRADA: 200 pts.

Ajuntament de Barcelona
Districte de les Corts

Title: **Activitats d'Infants Campaign**
Design Firm: Sonsoles Llorens, Barcelona, Spain
Art Director: Sonsoles Llorens
Designer: Sonsoles Llorens
Client: Ajuntament de Barcelona, Districte de les Corts

Only three vibrant colors are incorporated into each piece — and joins together hues you don't often see side-by-side — giving the overall effect of a carefree, multi-colored project. Bold lines are also used to promote a theater that caters to activities for children.

Title: Croatian Week in Bavaria Poster
Design Firm: Studio International, Zagreb, Croatia
Art Director: Boris Ljubicic
Designer: Boris Ljubicic
Client: The Ministry of Foreign Affairs of the
Republic of Croatia

Croatian Week is a celebration of culture, sport, tourism, and food in Munich, Bavaria, Germany. The Croatian visual identity is displayed in red and white squares, while the blue and white represent Bavaria. The resulting synthesis of colors and shapes create the unique event logo.

Title: The Woman in Black Poster Series
Design Firm: Hiromura Design Office, Tokyo, Japan
Art Director: Massaki Hiromura
Designers: Massaki Hiromura, Nobuhiko Aizawa
Client: Parco Co., Inc.

Scattered fingerprints connote intrigue in this "whodunit" poster that uses colors to enhance the mysterious mood of a far-away place.

New American Avantgarde Jazz

PIGPEN

Wayne Horvitz' New Band

Willisau

Freitag, 14. Januar 94

20.30 Uhr, Mohren

Wayne Horvitz keyboards

Briggan Krauss alto sax

Fred Chalenor bass

Mike Stone drums

Title: Pig Pen
Design Firm: Niklaus Troxler Design Studio,
Willisau, Switzerland
Art Director: Niklaus Troxler
Designer: Niklaus Troxler
Client: Jazz in Willisau

Conceived for an American alternate jazz group, the poster
displays all the single pieces of the U.S. flag arranged in a
playful montage.

Title: Horizon Healthcare 1993-94 Quarterly Reports
Design Firm: Vaughn/Wedeen Creative,
Albuquerque, New Mexico, USA
Art Director: Daniel Michael Flynn
Designer: Daniel Michael Flynn
Computer Production: Stan McCoy
Client: Horizon Healthcare Corporation

Computer illustrations, color choice, and type that's easy
on the eye help make profuse facts and figures accessible
and readable.

Title: Dead Trees Poster
Design Firm: Niklaus Troxler Design Studio,
Willisau, Switzerland
Art Director: Niklaus Troxler
Designer: Niklaus Troxler
Client: Niklaus Troxler

This stark poster was designed as a form of communication
that could be understood around the world — the grim results
of neglecting our environment. Says the designer, "The blood of
the trees shocks us all."

Jazzplakate von Niklaus Troxler
Kornhaus Burgdorf 27. Januar – 27. Februar 94

Title: Jazz Poster by Niklaus Troxler
Design Firm: Niklaus Troxler Design Studio,
Willisau, Switzerland
Art Director: Niklaus Troxler
Designer: Niklaus Troxler
Client: Kornhaus Burgdorf

The energy and electricity of jazz is telegraphed effectively
with bright paint splashes that combine to form a unified figure,
producing impeccable muscial chords and celebratory songs.

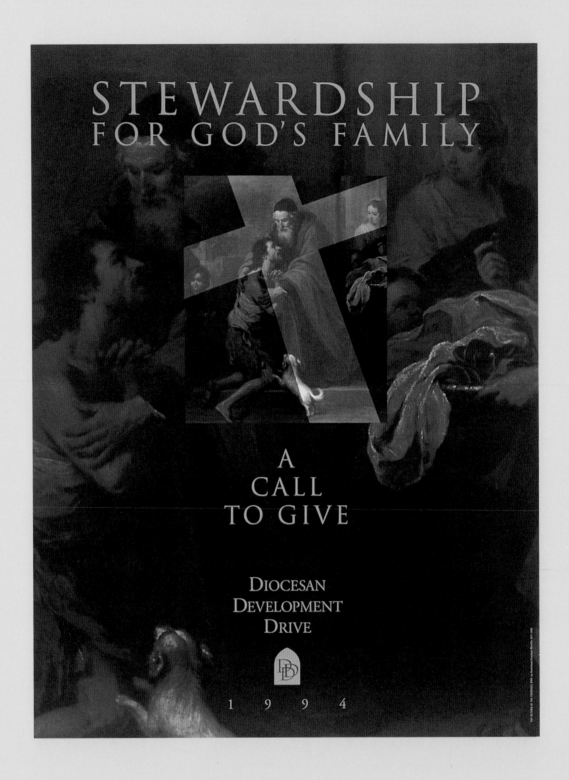

Title: Diocesan Development Drive Poster
Design Firm: Huddleston Malone Design Inc.,
Salt Lake City, Utah, USA
Art Director: Barry Huddleston
Designers: Todd Schofield, Barry Huddleston
Painter: Bartolomé Esteban Murillo (1617 - 1682)
Client: Diocesan Development Drive

The poster addresses not only the pious, but those who believe they have a responsibility towards the betterment of all people. The spiritual theme is underscored by the prominence of the cross symbol.

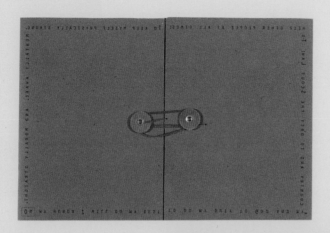

Title: Boy Scouts of America 1992/93 Annual Report
Design Firm: John Brady Design Consultants,
Pittsburgh, Pennsylvania, USA
Art Director: John Brady
Designer: Joseph Tomko
Photographer: Christopher Caffee
Client: Greater Pgh Council, Boy Scouts of America

This industrious annual report is bordered by the Boy Scouts'
motto and enhanced by captivating photos and vital facts
highlighted in yellow.

Title: Kison Stationery
Design Firm: Fleming Graphics Ltd.,
Vancouver, British Columbia, Canada
Art Director: Blair Pocock
Designer: Darren Bristol
Client: Kison & Associates

Development and human resources consultants, the company's slogan is "growth through learning," and both progress and altruism are paired on a complementary paper.

Title: Almond Brothers Logo
Design Firm: Sabin Design, San Diego, California, USA
Art Director: Bruce Ritter
Designer: Tracy Sabin
Client: Almond Board of California/Foote, Love, & Belding

This label boasts inspired use of only three colors, using a screen of the darker tan to achieve the lighter tan.

Title: Menus for Japanese Restaurant
Design Firm: Eymont Kin-Yee Hulett Pty Ltd,
Sydney, NSW, Australia
Art Director: Alison Hulett
Designer: Alison Hulett
Client: The ANA Hotel

A sense of charm and class without stuffiness is created with
these tassled menus that would undoubtedy enhance any
dining experience.

Title: Company Stationery
Design Firm: Wiley Designs,
Westlake Village, California, USA
Art Director: Caryn Wiley
Designer: Stephanie Powell
Client: Wiley Designs

To create attention, cut the business card in a shape that's
not quite rectangular, devise a new use for primary colors
and your initial, and keep the design clear and visible from
across the room.

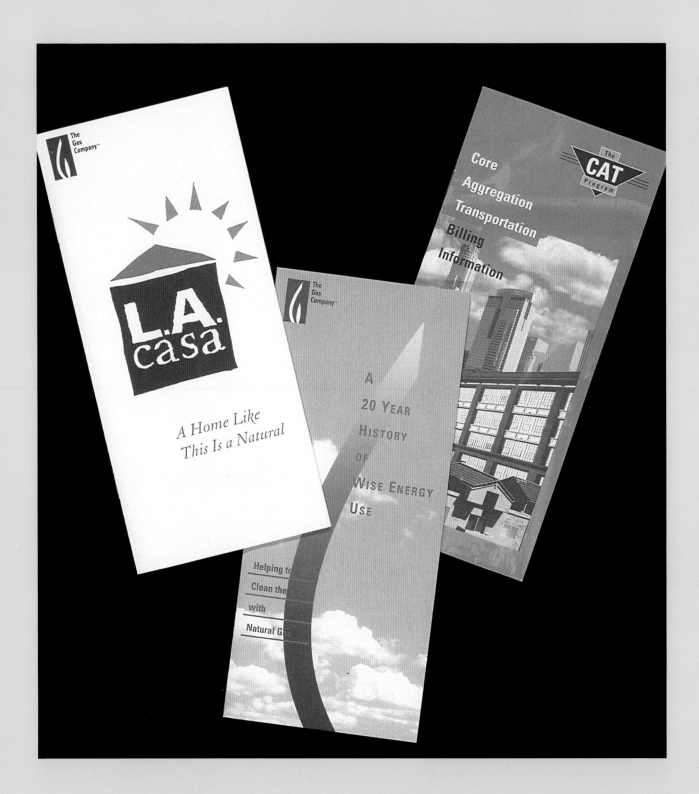

Title: Brochures: The Gas Company
Design Firm: Sussman/Prejza & Company, Inc.,
Culver City, California, USA
Art Directors: Debra Valencia, Deborah Sussman —
principal in charge
Designers: Ron Romero, Chris Pacione
Client: Southern California Gas Company

They are indeed three colors, no more. Limiting hues for each brochure but varying the colors used is an innovative technique that keeps costs low, but enriches the entire group of work.

Title: Love Magurou Book Jacket
Design Firm: Takashi Akiyama Studio, Tokyo, Japan
Art Director: Takashi Akiyama
Designer: Takashi Akiyama
Client: Creére Inc.

This exhilirating cover would be successful for its color choice alone, but it also sports a translucent paper band imprinted with fish icons to complete its winsome look.

Title: GTE Appreciation Lunch Invitation
Design Firm: SullivanPerkins, Dallas, Texas, USA
Art Directors: Ron Sullivan, Kelly Allen
Designer: Kelly Allen
Copywriters: Davy Woodruff, Hilary Kennard, Mark Perkins
Client: GTE

The paper is an important element for a three-color piece
that looks like several more. Text confined to a top banner
of color also complements the folksy design.

Title: **Luigi Pirandello Kaj je Resnica**
Design Firm: KROG, Ljubljana, Slovenia
Art Director: Edi Berk
Designer: Edi Berk
Photographer: Tone Stojko
Client: MGL (Town Theatre of Ljubljana)

The play is a satire on bourgeois morals where suspense, intrigue, and gossip abound and truth and playacting become indefinable. The powerful program cover depiction resounds with mania, alienation, and, surprisingly, hope.

Title: Manes Space Changes Flyer
Design Firm: Schowalter2 Design,
Short Hills, New Jersey, USA
Art Director: Toni Schowalter
Designer: Tim O'Donnell
Client: Manes Space

A move and a new employee can be dramatized when supported by minimal copy, deep coloring, and a measure of the unpredictable.

Title: The Wisdom of FDR Book Cover
Design Firm: Carol Publishing Group,
New York, New York, USA
Art Director: Steven Brower
Designer: Steven Brower
Illustrator: Steven Brower
Client: Carol Publishing Group

Whenever you doubt the potency of candor and clean lines, study this print piece; its showy colors and bright lettering guarantee conspicuousness. This piece plays with the form of a political poster, and uses red, white, and blue, but not the tones you may expect.

AUSTRALIA COUNCIL
Arts for Australians by Australians

Australia Council
for the Arts

Title: **Australia Council Booklet**
Design Firm: Spatchurst Design Associates,
Sydney, NSW, Australia
Art Director: Steven Joseph
Designer: Meryl Blundell
Client: Australia Council for the Arts

Lively logo elements are used as background in this
brochure's richly hued cover, synthesizing the Council's
mission with its membership and its commitment to freedom
in artistic expression.

25 YEARS YOUNG:

The Art Institute of

Fort Lauderdale

Title: Inside EMC Newsletter
Design Firm: EMC Marketing & Advertising, Inc.,
Pittsburgh, Pennsylvania, USA
Art Director: Vanessa Weber
Designer: Vanessa Weber
Client: EMC Marketing & Advertising, Inc.

Colors are at the forefront of a successful exercise to sustain interest in a group of varied stories and tantalize the readers of a diverse organization.

Title: Packaging for Spring Water
Design Firm: Eymont Kin-Yee Hulett Pty Ltd, Sydney, NSW, Australia
Art Director: Alison Hulett
Designer: Frank Chin
Client: Tradelink Pty Ltd

Solace emerges from cool, gentle colors as well as pure, placid lines. One can almost hear the refreshing stream of melted ice and taste the replenishing sweet drink.

Title: Deleo Clay Tile Sample Boxes
Design Firm: Mires Design, San Diego, California, USA
Art Director: Jose Serrano
Designer: Jose Serrano
Illustrator: Tracy Sabin
Client: Deleo Clay Tile

Using muted colors, these boxes impress the buyer with their contemporary style as well as their classic illustrations that create an atmosphere of southwestern country and uncomplicated living.

Title: DYE-NAMIX Business Papers Package
Design Firm: Wright Communications,
New York, New York, USA
Art Director: Nanette Wright
Designer: Janice Comes
Client: Raylene Marasco

A completely ingenious set of business papers for a dyeing
and painting studio, where stationery, invoice, envelope,
and business card are either odd-sized, use unexpected stock,
or come complete with fabric swatches.

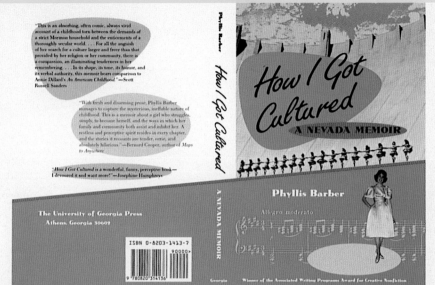

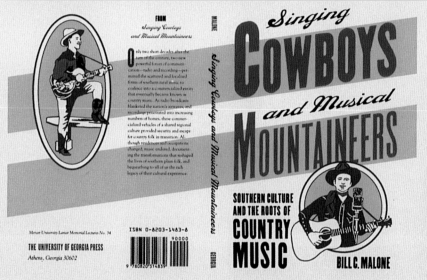

Title: Singing Cowboys and Musical Mountaineers and How I Got Cultured Book Jackets
Design Firm: The University of Georgia Press, Athens, Georgia, USA
Designer: Erin Kirk New
Client: University of Georgia Press

The "Singing Cowboys" jacket is rooted in old country music billboards and posters originating from Nashville. The design replicates the aged look of decades-old primary colors. "Cultured" was influenced by formica-type colors popular in the 1950s. The photo features the Rhythmettes, a dance troupe who performed at the Hoover Dam.

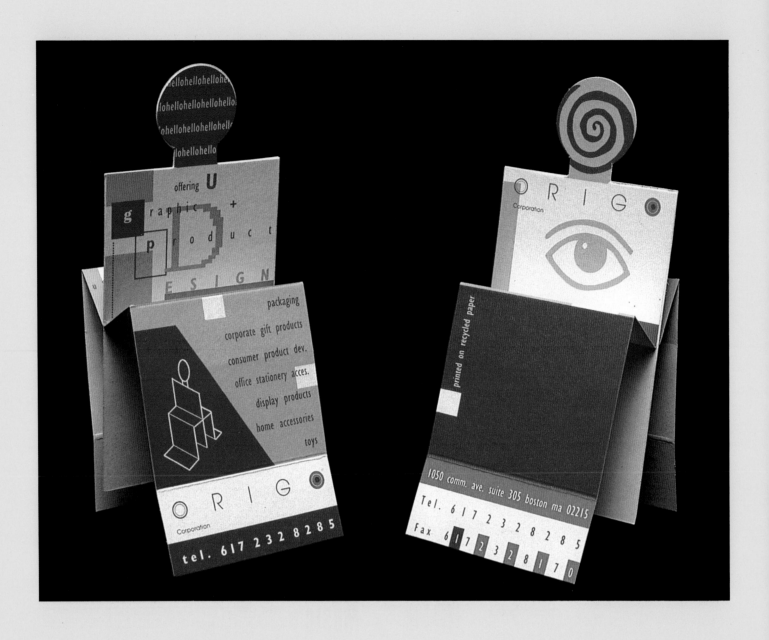

Title: Promotional Design
Design Firm: Origo Corporation, Boston, Massachusetts, USA
Art Director: Manidana Labbauf
Designer: Farsad Labbauf
Client: Origo Corporation

An attention-grabbing 3-D work that stands by itself and makes good use of stimulating colors, delivers pertinent information, and actually "speaks" to you.

Title: Young Imaginations Stationery
Design Firm: Sackett Design Associates,
San Francisco, California, USA
Art Director: Mark Sackett
Designer: Mark Sackett
Client: Young Imaginations

This concept appeals not only to young imaginations, but to every age. Feather-light with a delicate turn, it has captured the contents of dreams.

Title: Greenwich Hospital Aesthetic Surgery Brochure
Design Firm: The Q Design Group Ltd.,
Wilton, Connecticut, USA
Art Director: Susan Caldwell
Designer: Susan Caldwell
Photographer: Michael Heintz
Client: Greenwich Hospital

A considerate, gentle portrayal of aesthetic services using muted tones and photography that relates closely to the text, this is an excellent example of nuance and innuendo.

INTERNATIONAL YOUTH FOUNDATION

1991

Annual

Report

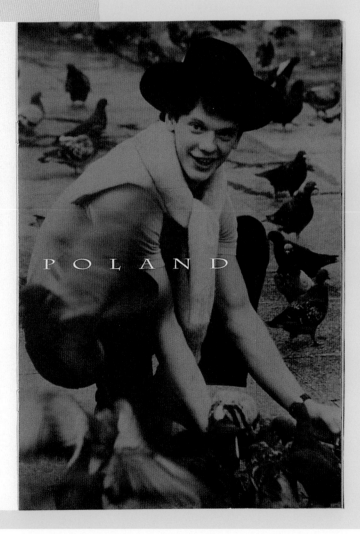

As Polish leaders analyze the current situation and develop strategies for the future, there is an emerging role for community-based programs and a commitment to see their efforts not only strengthened, but expanded.

Country Partner Summary/POLAND

Facilitating A New Society

Hope and aspirations abound as Poland faces an historic opportunity to forge a new society. The world watches while Poland struggles through the transition to a market economy and democratic society. Building a new nation demands both thoughtful planning and investing in human potential and capacity.

Poland's children & youth - the next generation of policy makers, business leaders, and parents - are key to realizing its newfound potential. Yet many are disillusioned and fearful of the future. As social and economic changes challenge tradition, there is a need to establish new opportunities through which young people can build their future. Key issues that require attention include:

Alienation. Polish youth experience severe alienation from their parents' society, and often among themselves as well. Combined with economic fears, an unresponsive school environment, and an absence of youth-oriented community support services, Polish youth experience severe struggles in their transition from adolescence to adulthood.

Educational Reform. While education is obligatory through secondary school, insufficient facilities result in overcrowded and tense classrooms, with sessions being conducted three shifts a day. Centered on a curriculum with little practical application, and very little interaction, there is a critical need to replace traditional hierarchical methods with greater youth participation; developing interpersonal skills, nurturing self-esteem, and encouraging peer support.

Unemployment. The transformation from a centrally-controlled to a market-driven economy has brought widespread unemployment. In January 1991, only 55,000 were reported unemployed; by year's end, more than two million were out of work. Preliminary estimates indicate that 53% of the students currently enrolled in trade schools will be unemployed upon graduation.

Environment. Almost one-third of Poland's population lives in ecologically endangered areas where air, soil and water pollution significantly exceed international standards.

Cultural Tolerance. Poland's regions are not only geographically defined, they are also culturally distinct. This fosters rivalry and prejudice among the various ethnic groups.

Integrating Handicapped Children into Society. Approximately eight percent of Poland's young people are handicapped. In addition to facing severe shortages of medicine and therapy, they are almost totally isolated from their peers and society.

As Polish leaders analyze the current situation and develop strategies for the future, there is an emerging role for community-based programs and a commitment to see their efforts not only strengthened, but expanded.

12

POLAND

Title: IYF 1991 Annual Report
Design Firm: Michael Hudson, Ltd., Minneapolis, Minnesota, USA
Art Director: Michael Hudson
Designers: Michael Hudson, Steve Pikala
Client: International Youth Foundation

This was a marketing showpiece for the foundation, as well as an annual report. The metallic colors were chosen for their youthfulness, earthiness, and ability to project credibility.

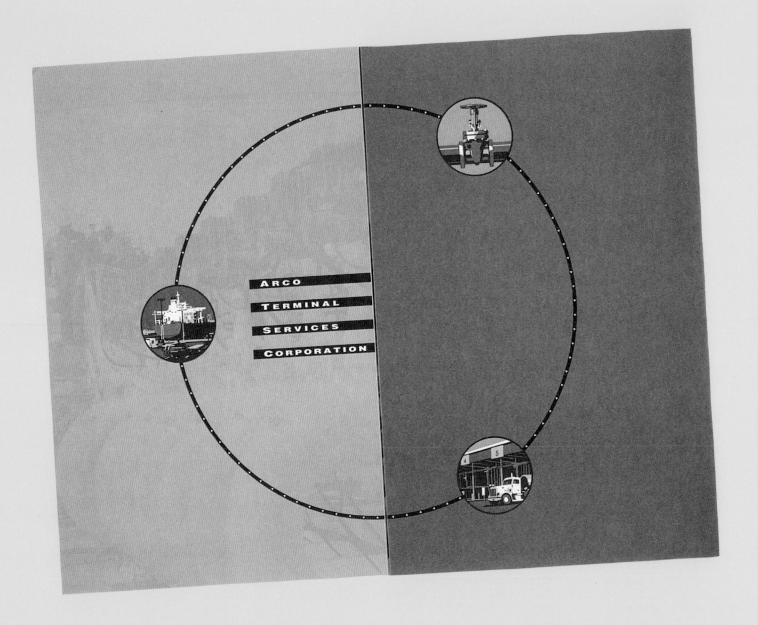

Title: Arco Terminal Services Brochure
Design Firm: White Design, Long Beach, California, USA
Art Director: John White
Designer: Aram Youssefian
Client: Arco Terminal Services

Imaginative folds that reveal bulletted information and
photographs make this graphic brochure communicate
technical information usefully.

Title: Constructing Iowa's Future Promotion
Design Firm: Sayles Graphic Design, Des Moines, Iowa, USA
Art Director: John Sayles
Designer: John Sayles
Copywriter: LuAnn Harkins
Client: Associated General Contractors

A commanding project needs something extraordinary in order to live up to its description. These pieces used verve and assertiveness to affect that posture, but very little color.

Title: WITS T-Shirt
Design Firm: University of Illinois at Urbana-Champaign, Champaign, Illinois USA
Designer: Nan Goggin
Client: Women, Information Technology, and Scholarship group at University of Illinois

WITS wanted something fun and a little on the loud side. Purple is the group color, and the organization of elements and colors suggests excitement and diversity. The shirt was designed to promote the group when it was worn at conferences.

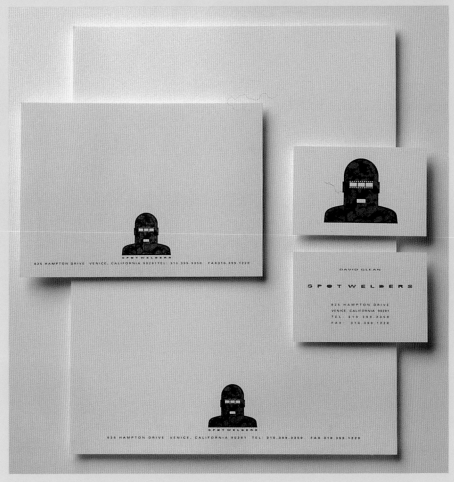

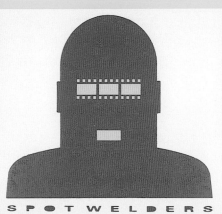

Title: Spot Welders Logo and Stationery Design
Design Firm: Jay Vigon Studio, Studio City, California, USA
Art Director: Jay Vigon
Designer: Jay Vigon
Client: Spot Welders Film Production Company

An original rendering of a unique company name is just as effective in different colors, different sizes, and for different applications.

Title: University of Dallas Annual Report
Design Firm: Joseph Rattan Design, Dallas, Texas, USA
Art Director: Joe Rattan
Designers: Greg Morgan, Joe Rattan
Photographer: Mike Haynes
Client: University of Dallas

Here's a lofty perspective of the distinguished faculty of a southern university. The black-and-white cover and subtle colors inside lend gentility to the piece.

INDICES OF 1·2&3 COLORS

Purple
252

Blue
276

CLIENT INDEX

DESIGN FIRM INDEX

Pat Taylor is Pat Taylor Inc., a one-man corporation specializing in logotypes and magazine design and production. Established in 1969 in Appleton, Wisconsin, Taylor moved to Washington, D.C. in 1971 to concentrate on magazines and other printed material. Taylor has received awards in graphic design from numerous Art Directors Clubs, as well as the Typographers International Association, Society of Publication Designers, National Composition Association, The Ozzie Awards, AIGA50, and International Logos & Trademarks Design Awards. His work has been published in Japan, Mexico, and the United States. Taylor has lectured on design at the Smithsonian Institution and at various colleges and universities.

Yellow
139

Blue
260